THE NEW POPULISM

Kathryn, LaDonna, and Fred Harris

FRED HARRIS

To the people. They endure.

THORP SPRINGS PRESS

BOOKS BY FRED R. HARRIS

The New Populism
Now Is the Time: A New Populist Call to Action
Alarms and Hopes: A Personal Journey, a Personal View
Report of the Commission on the Cities in the '70's
co-authored with John V. Lindsay
Social Science and National Policy
edited by Fred R. Harris

Portions of Chapter VIII first appeared as an article, "The Frog Hair Problem," in the May, 1972, issue of *Harper's* Magazine. Grateful acknowledgment is expressed for permission to reprint this material here.

"Sixteen Tons": Copyright 1947 by Hill and Range Songs, Inc., Elvis Presley Music, Inc., Gladys Music, Inc., and Noma Music, Inc. All rights administered by Hill and Range Songs, Inc. Used by permission.

"You Gotta Fight That Line" is recorded on Collector Records by Joe Glazer. Copyright © 1971 by Joe Glazer. Used by permission.

Published in cloth by Saturday Review Press
and in Canada by Doubleday Canada Ltd. $6.95

Photos: Lou Dematteis

Copyright © 1973 by Fred R. Harris

Library of Congress Catalog Card Number: 72–88653

ISBN 0–914476–50–5

This edition in paperback $2.00 published by

THORP SPRINGS PRESS
2311-C Woolsey Street
Berkeley, California 94705

Contents

Acknowledgments

I might never have become a populist except for the commonsense, naturally antigovernment feelings of my father, Fred B. Harris, who is a farmer living near Hastings, Oklahoma.

I owe more to friends than I can express. And to too many to list. A great many people have helped over the years to educate me, particularly in my home state. Oklahoma people are a kind of composite of America, and it was both a joy and a challenge to represent them for eight years in the United States Senate.

Most of all, I owe a great deal to my staff. My former legislative aide, James C. Rosapepe, is the best populist I know. And Sherry Jones, John Twohey, Steve Ristow, Bill Combs, Ann Chase, Charles William Maynes, and Shirley Coffield have all shared in inspiring these ideas and in helping to develop the New Populism.

Invaluable assistance has been given, too, by other staff members, including Jim Monroe, Gary Dage, Burl Hays, Ruth Matthews, Ella Mae Horse, Stella Jackmon, Christina Reichert, Thomas Latta, Constance Butler, Barbara Thompson, and Beverly Nation.

I want to express, of course, special appreciation to my wife, LaDonna. She is the only one I can say for sure agrees with *all* the viewpoints set forth in this book, because we virtually grew up together and helped to form each other's opinions.

PROLOGUE

Up with Those Who're Down

I grew up in Oklahoma during the Depression years, the 1930s. Franklin Roosevelt's background was radically different from that of my sharecropping, common-labor family.

Yet we identified with Roosevelt. More than that, we revered him. I think of his *voice* first—on the radio. We *watched* the radio in those days. We didn't just listen. We sat around it and watched the radio, and we often heard Franklin Roosevelt's voice—reassuring, hopeful.

Later, I saw his face in newsreels—confident, determined, jolly. He was busy. He was doing things; he was changing things. And God knows we needed things done and things changed.

There was no need to waste your time telling us of any flaws in his program. We didn't want to hear it. We did not believe it. (We didn't even believe he was crippled. My mind told me he was, but I am still shocked today to see pictures that actually show it.)

We were for Franklin Roosevelt because he was for us. And he was against those who were against us. He didn't pussyfoot around about it. He called them "malefactors of great wealth." And worse.

What is happening (has happened) to the old Roosevelt Coalition? That's become the favorite parlor-game question of political writers. It was a coalition of poor and working-class blacks and whites, farmers and intellectuals. Can such groups be held together no longer?

I grew up thinking "Okie" was a derogatory word, a slur. It was a long time before I read *The Grapes of Wrath*, because everybody I knew in Oklahoma said, "Old John Steinbeck just tried to make us look bad." Years later, an Oklahoma governor started a campaign to build "Okie" into a term of pride, as Negroes had done with "black." I like that. And I wish *The Grapes of Wrath* were required reading in our schools. It would teach people something about how to keep body and soul together in hard times. We'd learn that by ourselves none of us has the power to win out.

In a lush farming valley in California, once, I campaigned for the Democratic party's candidates. "I can't understand these Okies here," a local official told me. "I remember thirty years ago they came in here and lived in old car bodies; today, they are some of the strongest supporters George Wallace has."

Had they changed? Had Democratic liberalism changed? Had the times changed? Was it a flaw in them or a failure in the appeal? During the last several years I've tried to think out more clearly the answers to those questions.

While I was wondering about Okies, a friend of mine was wondering about Italian-Americans. Monsignor Geno Baroni of the U.S. Catholic Conference, now doing ground-breaking work among white ethnics, has gone through a process similar to mine. In the early 1960s he was in the forefront of the civil rights movement in America. But, before long, some black people began to say to him, "What are you doing down here with us? We don't want you. We can run *our* affairs ourselves. White people are the majority in this country; they have the power. They can change things, not us. So why don't you leave us alone and go work with your own kind?" This hurt.

But it began to make sense, too. He became more conscious that some of his own people, Italian coal-mining families in Pennsylvania, while they loved him, derided his work with "the niggers in Washington." There was obviously something wrong with his message, or his approach, if he couldn't even convince his own family.

I had a similar realization when I served as a member of the Kerner Commission, which looked into the awful riots that ignited so many of our cities in the fearsome summer of 1967. We rightly reported that racism and black people's feelings of powerlessness were the root causes of the violence.

One year later, things were one year worse. Three years later, I served as co-chairman of the Commission on the Cities in the Seventies of the National Urban Coalition. Things were *three* years worse.

"We've been talking to you politicians for five or six years, and still nothing gets done," a black woman told me in Atlanta.

She was right. Things are not better. They are worse —for both blacks and whites. Housing is worse. Health care delivery is worse—it's harder to get a doctor or to get into a hospital. Health costs are worse—it's harder to pay for needed medical attention. Education is worse. Unemployment is worse. Crime is worse.

Ringing appeals to conscience, to join together against

"the common enemies of man," have not been very effective.

A good many people unfortunately perceived the Kerner Commission message to be: "You should, out of the goodness of your heart and because of your Christian duty, pay more taxes to help poor black people in Detroit."

Their response was, "Bullshit! I've got enough troubles of my own. I'm barely making a living, and I'm already paying too much tax."

If I needed any further demonstration, this showed me that you can't have a mass movement without the masses.

As chairman of the Democratic National Committee in 1969, I had already been forced to think about that. Kevin Phillips was writing in *The Emerging Republican Majority* that the more the Democratic party worried about the problems of black people, poor people, and the people of the central cities, the more it would drive the rest of the people into the Republican party. That did not seem morally right to me, and I did not want it to be true.

It began to become clear to me that you can't appeal to black people and poor people and the people of the central cities on the basis of their own self-interest and to everybody else on the basis of morality. That kind of an appeal is the luxury of the intellectual elite—for people who are, themselves, socially and economically secure.

Instead of trying to convert people, you have to think again about why we are banded together as an organized society.

It's instructive to study the Constitution and formal governmental system of even the most unstable Latin American "republic." It may look great in print, but things haven't worked out that way. The tax laws may sound all right, but nobody pays any attention to them.

Governments are more than their basic documents. The United States Constitution is, indeed, a splendid instrument, our system of representative government a marvel.

But they work because of the social contract that underlies them—because we have, in a way, agreed to live together in the same house and to share in duties and privileges on some kind of fair—not necessarily equal—basis. That applies to *all* the members of the society.

A few weeks after the terrible summer floods of 1972 in Pennsylvania, I saw HUD Secretary George Romney on television explaining why the government couldn't provide any greater and faster assistance to the wretched flood victims trying to live and rebuild. He was outraged when Governor Milton Shapp reminded him of how fast the government had come to the aid of Lockheed and Penn Central. Romney's response wasn't very persuasive: "Politics," he grouched.

Secretary Romney wound up the interview by calling on all Americans to send contributions to the Red Cross to help those who had lost their homes and belongings.

Now, nobody said those flood victims weren't deserving. Nobody said it was their own fault. Nobody said they weren't trying to help themselves. But here was their government, not thinking in terms of the *rights* of the victims, but in terms of appealing for voluntary charity to them. What kind of social contract is that?

There, exactly, is the problem with traditional liberalism, the flaw in "conscience" politics. Our society should not depend upon charity, not even charity by government. People want what's rightly theirs. It is that kind of system to which they thought they had assented.

Each American inherits our political system and history. His or her right to be a free person and to have an equal chance, economically and politically, is a part of the social contract that binds us together.

The social contract is threatening to tear apart. We see rising crime. Rising alcoholism. Rising use of narcotics. Rising violence and self-destructive behavior. Rising apathy and withdrawal. Rising anger and polarization between races and classes.

These are symptoms. Symptoms of a society in deep stress. And treating symptoms alone will not alleviate the stress.

In 1971 I visited a Chicano-run narcotics referral center in a storefront in Oakland, California. It's a neighborhood operation run by ex-addicts. That month alone, 147 people had voluntarily come in off the streets to be sent to a detoxification center.

I talked at some length with the terribly discouraged center workers. They agreed that heroin would not be so freely available except for considerable official corruption, but they said, "That's for you politicians to do something about." They uniformly made clear that the problem was much deeper.

"We're not so much interested in the supply," said one volunteer worker who had first become a heroin addict in San Quentin, where, he said, the drug was even more plentiful than on most city streets. "There's been heroin on the streets of Oakland ever since I can remember, and there always will be heroin—or something else.

"People walk in here looking for help. They go through the hell of detox and come out clean. But where can they go from there? They're back on the streets. They don't have any education. They can't get a job. They're hassled by the police.

"The first thing you know they're shooting up again, and when their habit builds back up to seventy-five or a hundred dollars a day, they're back here again looking for help.

"Man, we're not so much interested in the supply. We're interested in the *demand*. Something's gotta be done about the demand."

Similarly, most political solutions tend to deal only with the symptoms—and not the causes.

The problems of blacks and whites in America overlap to a considerable degree. Marshall Frady wrote in *Life* magazine in 1972 about Will D. Campbell, a Yale-educated Southern Baptist preacher in Nashville, Tennessee, who'd had to do a lot of the same hard thinking that Monsignor Baroni and I had done.

"Some of my black friends like Stokely Carmichael," he told Frady, "started telling me, 'Look here, man, we pretty much got things cool and together with *our* folks. If you want to help out real bad, why don't you go to work on *your* people!' I said, 'Man, you happen to be talking about red-necks—they'll *kill* me.' And he said, 'That sort of means they're the problem then, don't it?' "

Answering that question, Campbell began to spend a good part of his time with working-class Southern whites, and he began to see a parallel. "Whatever it is that's keeping the red-neck a Kluxer and the black man a nigger—whatever's keeping them outside and poor and without any hope—is the same thing for both," he said.

In some ways it's been more damaging for the white. "In a way, see," Campbell said, "the red-neck's been the special victim of the whole system. It took his head away. The system got about everything else from the black man —his back, a portion of his spirit maybe—but it never really managed to get his head. All along, the black man's known more or less what's been going on. But the red-neck—hell, he's never known who the enemy was. If you remember anything about the course of Populism, every time the poor white began getting together in natural alliance with the equally dispossessed black, he'd be told that it meant blacks were going to ravish his wimminfolks, and the Bolsheviks were going to invade the courthouse. He's never known how he's been had."

Monsignor Baroni found the same thing with urban white ethnics. Their interests have been ignored as much as have the interests of the blacks and the Southern whites.

In America we have both a race problem *and* a class problem. And each makes the other worse.

Racism *is* a central fact of American history—of human history for that matter. It is not a passing thing. It has been with us from the first, and it's still with us. Realizing that requires a wrenching change in white thinking. White history is what we've studied. The white experience is what we've lived. But there have been blacks—and other minorities—around all the time. They are still around, and we have been made painfully aware of it.

We cannot compromise on race. That's what we've always tried, and it's morally wrong. But, in addition to that, compromise is much too costly—in blood, in money, and in self-esteem.

Economic class is also a central fact of American history—again, of human history for that matter. Income, wealth, and ownership in America—and the power that goes with them—have become increasingly concentrated in fewer and fewer hands. We cannot compromise on that issue either.

But in recent years there has come to be a growing and justified distrust of government itself, and of politicians, and of the "programmatic" approach to basic problems.

The steelworker in Gary, the small farmer in Oklahoma, the Chicano mother in Los Angeles, the old person in Miami, the native American in Arizona, the teacher in Cleveland, the garbage worker in New York—

they all know that a little more housing, a little more job training, a few more food stamps, a few more summer jobs—though we need them all—will not do.

The traditional liberal approach is to look at old people who have nutritional problems and offer food stamps, or to look at old people who have housing problems and offer housing programs, or to look at old people who have health problems and offer Medicare. What most old people lack is money.

Farmers who have no economic security, black people who can't get into a building trades union, auto workers going mad with the dullness of their work—what they all lack is power.

And missing from all their lives, and the lives of many of us, is the integrating theme in our society that might give integrating worth to our existence.

When I was Democratic chairman, back in the fall of 1969, I began to speak about "the New Populism." I didn't know yet what that meant, totally, but I knew where it was headed. I knew that the New Populism had to deal with individual rights and individual power, as opposed to concentrated economic and political power. It had to deal with the problems of economic class, as well as with race. It had to deal with distrust of government. It had to deal with concentrated wealth and corporate power.

The New Populism—and it doesn't matter what you call it—means that most Americans are commonly exploited, but that, if we get ourselves together, we are a popular majority and can take back our government. It seeks to put America back together again—across the lines of race, age, sex, and region. Those in the coalition don't have to love each other. I wish they would. But all they have to do is recognize their common interests.

The New Populism promises a more stable, secure

society of self-esteem—for the rich as well as for the not so rich. Most of us will be willing to pay and sacrifice for that promise if we can be assured that, unlike in the past, what we pay and what we give will really make a difference.

The New Populism is against bigness, against concentrated economic and political power—whether it is in government, corporations, unions, or institutions.

The choice that will dominate the 1970s is a choice between individual liberty and power or greater governmental, corporate, and institutional power.

Our national goal, simply stated, should be:

—to distribute income and wealth more fairly;
—to deconcentrate economic and political power; and
—to make real the power and liberty of the people.

The *public* statement of this goal is vitally important. It will mean that, thereafter, governments, political parties, and politicians will regularly have to give an account of their stewardship in terms of this New Populist goal.

And the stated goal will supply some overall meaning to the work of ordinary politicians—trying to change a clause here or improve a program there. It will lend value to the way they spend their days.

This book is an attempt to update the New Populism and to give an overview of it. It doesn't try to provide an answer for everything. It doesn't, for example, say much about the critical problem of population growth—though there is strong evidence that a rise in income has more to do with a decrease in birthrate than anything else does. It doesn't attempt to deal with foreign policy —though the Ellsberg Pentagon Papers seem to indicate that a populist foreign policy, based upon the people's full knowledge and consent, would much more likely tend to be in tune with our professed ideals.

I've always believed that a senator has dual responsibilities: to work within the forum of which he is a member; and to try to change the climate within which the forum itself operates. I spent eight years in the United States Senate trying to do both. I want to spend most of my time now helping to change the public climate.

The civil rights movement, the women's movement, the ecology movement, the end-the-war movement—none of these were originated by politicians. They began as citizens' movements.

I once saw painted on a wall in a Latin American country: *"Arriba con los de abajo"*—"Up with those who are down." Not a bad slogan for a citizens' movement.

It's not a bad principle for a society.

CHAPTER

I

Take the Rich off Welfare

We ought to require economists to be able to recite from memory a couple of lines from Oliver Goldsmith:

> Ill fares the land, to hastening ills a prey,
> Where wealth accumulates, and men decay.

We're apt to think of the "dismal science" as merely working out an acceptable daily trade-off between the equal ills of unemployment and inflation. I'd like to see New Populist caucuses at all meetings of economists and political scientists.

Perhaps that would be one way to begin to get politicians and officials to see that the social problems of America will not be solved by what amounts to more handouts for the rich, but by more income for the people. People can buy health and housing and education—and some dignity, for that matter—if they have money. But that money is crucial. Advice will not suffice.

And money is what most Americans lack. When my mother used to make twenty-five cents an hour as a domestic, a dollar an hour seemed like a large wage to her. With that memory of what was once a "good wage," it's easy to forget what it actually costs to live in this day of inflated dollars and higher taxes.

So we point with pride to the sharp increases in median family income, which rose from around $5,000 in 1947 to around $9,500 in 1969, and we assume that workers are better off.

Wrong. Workers are worse off relative to what it costs to live and relative to what others in the economy have.

It is no good saying poor people in America are better off than poor people in Belgium. Or that working people in America are better off than working people in Spain. Or that black people in America are better off than black people in Tanzania.

Poor people and working people and black people in America are not Belgians or Spaniards or Tanzanians. They are Americans. It was an American social contract to which they agreed. And they have a right to judge their lives and their hopes by American standards.

Most Americans are not doing very well. According to the Bureau of Labor Statistics, an urban family of four today needs somewhat more than $10,000 a year to have just a "modest but adequate standard of living."

All but the most highly paid industrial workers earn incomes substantially less than that. As a matter of fact, 48.4 percent of all the *white* families in America earn less. And of those white families who do make more than that, many can do so only because both the husband and wife are working.

The fact is that after all our New Deal programs the upper one-fifth of our families now have 41 percent of the income—after taxes. The lower one-fifth has only 5 percent. That spread is slightly worse than it was in Franklin Roosevelt's day.

The distribution of wealth is worse than the distribution of income. Eight percent of our people own 60 percent of all the assets.

There's a widespread myth of a "people's capitalism" in America. However good it may sound, it's not true. There may be a lot of stockholders, but 80 percent of our productive capital is held by only 2.3 percent of American households, and 5 to 8 percent own the rest. Two percent of the people in America own 80 percent of all individually held corporate stock and 90 percent of all individually held corporate bonds.

Since most U.S. economic growth is in corporate capital and internally generated, it is simply wrong to assume that if the economic pie gets larger "everybody" will be better off. Instead, the maldistribution of wealth and ownership will grow.

For all of us, money decides whether we can send our kids to college or buy a home or get health care when we need it. And money is power.

The rule of primogeniture, a system by which the king's eldest son became king, went out of vogue a long time ago, even though some people justified it on the grounds that "we get a lot of bad kings that way, but it saves a lot of trouble." Yet today's rich—the Mellons, the Rockefellers, the Fords and Du Ponts—as well as the owners of great blocks of General Motors stock and other fortunes, pass from one generation to another more power over human lives than most of history's kings dared dream of.

This maldistribution of wealth and income continues despite the *tacit* understanding of a national goal to the contrary. What are supposedly graduated income and inheritance taxes, Social Security, health and housing programs, and minimum wage laws unless they are an attempt at a more fair distribution of wealth and income? We *seem* to be for it.

That being so, why have we done so poorly at it? Partly because of a kind of chamber-of-commerce boosterism in our thinking: "Rich folks have to get richer so that the rest of the folks can have jobs." Yet Japan, with the most rapid rate of economic growth of any country in the world, also has the most equal distribution of pretax income. The ratio of the income of its upper one-fifth to its lower one-fifth is only five to one, compared with eight to one in the United States.

The real reason why income and wealth are so concentrated in this country is that fair distribution is an unstated goal, not an *explicit* one.

There is no regular publication of distribution indicators, and, until very recently, almost nothing was written on the subject by academicians. Neither the executive nor the legislative branch of the federal government makes any attempt at all to discover the effect on distribution of its programs or policies.

We're hampered by the "Scrooge Syndrome," which still characterizes too much of traditional liberalism: every now and then we are shocked into taking a turkey to the Cratchits at Christmas, when decent wages all year long would have worked better.

Economic justice should not depend solely upon government programs. Bureaucracy tends to grow, according to Parkinson's law. It also tends to become charity-oriented, and it tends to become removed and isolated from its clients.

The New Populism is not so much a program as it is a process. It calls more for government action than for government administration. That means, among other things, that we ought always ask one question of any new program being considered or any old program under review: is there a way to accomplish the same result by giving the money to the people directly?

Take training programs. Some of them are good, obviously, but I doubt that it can be shown that anyone was ever trained into a job where the job did not exist. Yet, every time unemployment goes up, there is a big push to set up more training programs.

The best way for people to get money is by working. A private job is best, because it doesn't depend upon an annual act of Congress. But there are plenty of things that need to be done in our society, and a fundamental responsibility of government is to see that everyone willing and able to work has a job at decent pay.

For those who can't work or who can't find work, there ought to be a decent income. On a visit to a housing project for old people in Miami, my wife and I talked with an old man who said, "I've got cataracts on both eyes, and I can't shop anymore or cook my own food. Why can't I take my food stamps to the restaurant and buy prepared food?"

Well, why can't he? Even better, why couldn't he just have the money—and the options and power over his own life that go with money?

I'm convinced that a negative income tax is the best income-maintenance system. Everybody would fill out the same form; some would pay in, and some would receive. It would be the least demeaning system. It would require the least machinery to administer. And its distributive effect would be obvious and easily calculated.

The impact on distribution should be a key measurement to gauge the effectiveness of every public expenditure.

Consider education, surely a basic public responsibility. Education has generally been understood to be the most effective way for a person in our society to rise from one economic class to another.

This doesn't always work. Professor David Mundel at Harvard has done a careful analysis of federal subsidies for higher education. He shows, first of all, that most of these subsidies are channeled through institutions, rather than through students, and that the more prestigious colleges and universities in each state, those most likely to be attended by students from upper-income families, are the ones most heavily subsidized. The study shows that the net effect of all federal subsidization of higher education is to assist most those who need it least. Students from low-income families receive the benefit of subsidies averaging less than two-thirds of the money given students from families with incomes of more than $30,000 a year. In every instance, the federal higher education subsidy *increases* as family income increases.

Here we have a program laudable in principle but more than questionable in effect. We start out trying to equalize opportunity, regardless of class. We wind up hardening class lines, giving additional advantage to those who were born advantaged. We provide greater opportunity for increased income and wealth to those who already have it. One would think that, at the very least, government should refrain from redistributing income and wealth in the wrong direction.

But most of our subsidies don't even start out with so laudable a purpose. In 1832 Andrew Jackson said:

When the laws undertake . . . to make the rich richer and the potent more powerful, the humble members of society—the farmers, mechanics, and laborers—who have neither the time nor the means of securing like favors to themselves, have a right to complain of the injustice of their government.

Fred R. Harris

There's no telling what Jackson would say today if he knew that federal subsidies for private gain play the part in modern politics that patronage and graft did in the nineteenth century. Subsidies are the lifeblood—tainted, to be sure—of the modern political process.

In the nineteenth century, government involvement in economic affairs was but a shadow of what it is today. There were financial advantages to be gained if a particular party controlled the Congress or the Presidency—congressional land grants for building the railroads, for example. But the real lure of political life was the spoils system. When a party captured the White House or the Congress, there were jobs aplenty for all those who had helped out in the campaign. The old rascals were thrown out so that the new rascals could move in.

Civil service reform largely changed that. But still many of our historians and journalists are suffering from a kind of historical hangover. Assuming the old-style spoils system still exists, they continue to focus on who gets what job in the wake of political victory and how that particular job is used or abused for financial gain.

Meanwhile, the real raid on the treasury—which makes mere graft pale by comparison and which seems to survive party changes—takes place largely unheeded.

Senator William Proxmire's Joint Economic Committee of the Congress began in 1972 the first study *ever* done of federal subsidies—and it showed $63 billion worth of them, not counting welfare and Social Security and not even counting the subsidizing effect for industry of federal regulation, licensing, and import quotas.

Commenting on the strange fact that nobody—not Congress, not economists or political scientists—had paid much attention to this uneven distribution of such massive public funds, one-fourth of the federal budget, and on the meaning of the Proxmire findings, Taylor

The New Populism

Branch wrote in the *Washington Monthly* that the folklore of capitalism has apparently wiped the idea of a handout to business from the minds of economic scholars. He said that the Proxmire study found *de facto* socialism and a fundamentally inequitable formula for socialist distribution.

By means of such subsidies the federal government generally intervenes in the marketplace on the side of—you guessed it—those least entitled to the intervention.

A basic tenet of Democratic liberalism is that the little farmer is important in America, and I believe this is true. But the federal government has almost helped the little farmer out of existence. Money voted in his name doesn't wind up in his pocket. Former Budget Director Charles Schultze has shown that the one-half of the farm population with the lowest income gets only around 9 percent of the federal farm subsidy, while the upper one-fifth gets nearly 63 percent.

The federal government takes $10 billion in public money and redistributes it in the form of farm subsidies. What happens? If you are one of the richer 7 percent of farmers who make an average of $13,400 a year, you get another $14,000. If, on the other hand, you are one of those 40 percent of American farmers scratching out an average of a bare $800 a year, you get only $300.

Franklin Roosevelt vetoed a special tax subsidy for timber producers, but the Congress passed it, and it's still in effect, costing the taxpayers, all of us, around $140 million a year now. One hundred million dollars of that goes to just five corporations: Boise Cascade, Georgia-Pacific, International Paper, U.S. Plywood, and Weyerhaeuser. That is not only government redistribution of wealth and income in the wrong direction, it is also—as is so often the case—bad social policy, allowing pulpwood, for example, to compete unfairly with recycled paper.

How does Congress get talked into these subsidies—
or talked into keeping them? Taylor Branch, specifically
citing Jeremy J. Warford's *Public Policy Toward General
Aviation,* has broken down the lobbying arguments into
four main categories.

There are 130,000 airplanes in America, excluding
military aircraft. Ninety-eight percent of them are private
or business airplanes. The rest belong to the airlines.
About three-fourths of the takeoffs and landings at publicly built airports, controlled by publicly financed FAA
towers and personnel, are by private and business airplanes. The owners of these private craft receive the
benefit of about $500 million a year in federal subsidies
for such things as traffic control and airport construction, and another $140 million in other kinds of state and
local subsidies. In addition, more than three-fourths of
the cost of all flights by these private and business airplanes is deducted for tax purposes as a business expense.

Not many people own their own planes, and those
who do certainly wouldn't argue for their right to receive these subsidies from the rest of us on the outright basis that it's cheaper to get it from the public
treasury than it is to pay for it themselves. They're
against socialism. Instead, of course, they have arguments for these subsidies in terms of the public interest, as they see it from their special vantage point
high in the sky:

Highest Common Denominator. This argument goes: every other mode of transportation is subsidized; why
shouldn't ours be? The effect of this argument is always
to add on more subsidies, never take any away.

Don't Hurt the Little Guy. This argument goes: if they
had to pay their own way, most ordinary people couldn't
do it without government help. Despite the fact that only

one-half of 1 percent of all Americans fly their own planes, and most of these flights are tax-deductible, this argument somehow gets a hearing.

Extraordinary Public Benefits. This argument goes: the country as a whole benefits from this use of public funds, not just the recipients. The aviation lobby says, "General aviation helps to arrest the decline of sparsely populated regions." There must be a better way to do it.

National Defense. This argument goes: our country is stronger because of this use of the people's money. Aviation says, "It would be a major advantage to the Communist plan if we were to eliminate the vast facilities and national defense capabilities of general aviation's fleet of over 110,000 planes." We need to be ready to let 'em have it with our Lear Jets and Cessnas.

Mostly, though, the arguments do not even have to be made. The subsidies are already on the books, and there is no system for regularly reviewing them.

Then how does it really work? How *is* the system perpetuated? The favored group—the airplane owners, say—decides to take 1 percent of its $500 million subsidy and put together a war chest of $5 million to elect and reelect its friends.

The lobby spends its war chest to elect its friends. Its friends get elected by using the money to tell us what a good job they're doing. When they get back in office, they vote the subsidy again.

The examination of that political cycle would probably be at least as revealing as the attention economists now give to macroeconomic fiscal and monetary policies.

Those who pay the dues required by a society's social contract have a right to expect fair treatment in return. But what if the dues themselves are unfair? Then one has a right to ask, what *is* fair?

"The Fred B. Harris Memorial Library" is a sign that

will never be hung. Not because my father isn't as charitable as other people. He just doesn't have it to give. One reason is that he pays a disproportionate share of the dues that run our society.

People like him have been taught to dislike welfare programs. Now they're beginning to see that there's a lot of welfare that goes by a different name.

It doesn't matter that we *say* that taxes ought to be based upon the ability to pay. You can be a worker in GM's Vega plant in Lordstown, Ohio, making $9,000 a year for turning the same screw 107 times an hour, having to hold up your hand to go to the toilet and slip around to take a smoke. Or you can be Richard Gerstenberg, the chairman of GM, with all your country clubs, corporate jets, and plush offices, making close to one million dollars a year in salary, incentives, and investments. You still pay at the same rate—roughly 33⅓ percent—in total local, state, and federal taxes. There's not much progressive taxation in that, and people know it.

One hundred and twenty-two Americans with incomes over $200,000 paid no federal income tax in 1970; 730,000 families with incomes over $10,000 also paid no tax. These are shocking facts.

The federal corporate income tax is set by law at 48 percent. Yet the twenty-six largest oil companies in America paid federal income tax of only 7.5 percent in 1969. And things are getting even worse. In 1970, out of nearly 1.7 million corporations, 725,986—or 43 percent of American corporations—paid no federal income tax. U.S. Steel, the twelfth largest corporation, with $5 billion annual business, paid zero federal income tax. And, in 1971, there were five American corporations with combined earnings in excess of $375 million that got off scot free.

The best profit year for American corporations in five

years was 1971, but, as Congressman Charles A. Vanik of Ohio has pointed out, some of the largest corporations—Continental Oil, McDonnell Douglas, Gulf + Western Industries, Aluminum Company of America, and Signal Companies—paid no federal income tax in that year.

An assistant secretary of the Treasury appeared before the Joint Economic Committee of the Congress in 1972 to defend this system. He cited statistics to show that people with large incomes pay sizable percentages of their "taxable income." But Congressman Henry Reuss of Wisconsin wouldn't let him get away with that, and he made the Treasury official admit under questioning that the phrase "taxable income" is precisely the problem. It is a figure arrived at only after taking advantage of tax loopholes, such as those for capital gains, oil and gas depletion, and tax-free municipal bonds.

In a society that rightly pays tribute to the "work ethic" (which President Nixon seems to mention in about every third speech), it is more than strange that we should tax income earned by the work of working people much more heavily than we do income earned from investments.

If you make your living from Ford stock that goes up in value, rather than from working harder to produce more Fords, you get a bonus under the capital gains provision of the tax laws.

And the tax laws favor bigness. As former Congressman Abner J. Mikva has shown, the legal rate for all corporations is 48 percent, but the average *effective* tax rate for American corporations in 1969 was only 37 percent. The bigger you get, the better it gets. The average tax rate for the biggest one hundred American industrial corporations was only 29.9 percent. Some of the largest banks enjoy a tax rate of only 16 percent.

The smaller companies, then, were obviously paying a rate higher than the average—they were paying around 44 percent.

ITT in 1969, as pointed out by Congressman Mikva, had a net income before federal income taxes of about $360 million, and it paid on an effective tax rate that year of something over 14 percent. As it grew, its tax rate shrunk. After bringing other companies into its conglomerate web, ITT's net income before federal taxes had grown to $410 million by 1970, but its effective tax rate had dwindled to only about 5 percent.

The Sixteenth Amendment to the United States Constitution authorized a tax on income "from whatever source," and, as has been stated by Phillip M. Stern, author of *The Great Treasury Raid,* if oil-rich Jean Paul Getty paid tax on his income "from whatever source," the U.S. Treasury would be better off by about $70 million a year.

Instead, Mr. Getty pays only a few thousand dollars. That's what President Kennedy told two senators in the early sixties.

Mr. Stern points out that the rest of U.S. taxpayers have to make up that $70 million, the same as if it were paid to Mr. Getty directly out of the federal treasury. The 200,000 richest families in the country escape an estimated $13.7 billion a year in federal income taxes through the capital gains loopholes alone. The rest of us, in effect, foot the bill. I call that welfare for the rich.

Bringing about tax fairness will require a nationwide citizens' movement.

The sentiment is there. A few of us hurriedly put together a fight for a minority platform plank on tax reform at the Democratic National Convention in 1972 after the Platform Committee adopted one with all the clout of a wet noodle. The minority proposal called for:

—Repeal of existing personal income tax laws.

—Enactment of a sharply graduated personal income tax providing for equal taxation of all income no matter what the source of that income.

—Provision for an income tax credit for each dependent to replace, and fully compensate for, current personal income tax exemptions and deductions of benefit to the average taxpayer, such as home mortgage interest and medical deductions.

—Replacement of existing hidden tax subsidies with direct payments where such subsidies are determined to serve a vital national interest, such as financing of state and local bonds and building low-income housing.

—Complete revision of the corporate income tax laws to eliminate all loopholes and to provide for graduated rates to ease the burden on small business.

For our trouble, we got massive lobbying against us from some of George McGovern's more overzealous operatives (one was quoted as saying adoption of the minority plank would cost the campaign $5 million in contributions). And there was a Dempsey-Tunney bad count from the chair. Even so, we clearly got a majority vote from the first democratically selected delegates ever to attend a national party convention. And the "ayes" heard from the Wallace section were as strong as those from the rest of the hall. There is a New Populist coalition that can be put together.

But the obstacles are enormous. And they are centered in the Senate Finance Committee and the House Ways and Means Committee.

It was the late senator from Louisiana Huey P. Long who said:

We are not doing the greatest good to the greatest number when we let the few dominate us in government, finance and industry, and allow the great masses of our people to become the political serfs and industrial slaves of super-lords of finance.

His son, Russell Long, is today chairman of the Senate Finance Committee, and it is no exaggeration to say that he views such "share-the-wealth" ideas with something less than enthusiasm.

I quit going to the Senate Finance Committee early in 1972 after the committee refused to open its meetings to the public. I preferred to take my chances in the full Senate.

In committee, it's a lot easier to adopt Magnolia Oil Company's special tax break (as the committee did when considering the investment tax credit law) in a private club atmosphere of "I'll support your amendment if you'll support mine," without the prying eyes of the taxpayers.

The operation of the House Ways and Means Committee is even more susceptible to private interest action. Once or twice a year, the committee has a "members' day" when each member is given a chance to offer at least one tax bill for regular adoption.

On the House floor, a closed rule usually prevents amendments to tax bills by individual House members. They are required to vote "yes" or "no" on a total tax package that may be—and most often is—a bundle of special tax advantages for everybody but the average working person.

It is not surprising that every new attempt at tax justice seems to be taken over by the rich and corporate interests.

In 1969 the Congress passed what it was pleased to

call the "Tax Reform Act." The effect was not quite as good as the name. For example, the Congress voted $15 million a year in tax inducement for cleaning up the environment. As usual, it never paused to calculate the distributive effect.

And, as a couple of tax lawyers at Boston University have shown, the distributive effect worked in the wrong direction. Their study showed that from an expenditure of $150,000 for a certified pollution control facility, the richest corporations benefit most. If a company's profits are more than $25,000, it gets for that $150,000 investment a tax advantage of nearly $12,000. If its profits are below $25,000, it gets a tax advantage of only around $5,500 or less. If it has no profits at all, or if it changes its practices to reduce pollution without a capital expenditure, such as deciding to use low-sulfur fuel, it gets no tax benefit.

In 1971 billions of dollars' worth of tax cuts were voted for big business. Secretary of the Treasury John Connally appeared before the Senate Finance Committee and successfully lobbied for tax cuts for business amounting to more than $16 billion over a three-year period—an investment tax credit and an accelerated depreciation system, already mostly implemented by administrative order—to encourage increased corporate expenditures for the purchase and building of more plant and machinery. This was supposed to result in an increased number of jobs.

At the time, I said to Secretary Connally that his plan reminded me of Rube Goldberg's inventions. Goldberg was a genius in dreaming up absurdly complex ways of accomplishing simple things.

The idea of these tax advantages for business and industry was to encourage them to spend more for machines, so that more people would be hired to make the machines, so that these people with new jobs would spend more money on business products, so that business profits would go up. We would have been better off to give tax cuts for ordinary taxpayers in the first place.

Secretary Connally—and the Congress—decided upon this huge tax subsidy for business, despite the fact that at the time one-fourth of existing American plant capacity was already idle, instead of giving some or all of this tax reduction to ordinary Americans, thereby stimulating the demand for business products directly, rather than indirectly.

When the Congress is voting tax changes, the tendency is to enact new loopholes to compensate for old loopholes, rather than to eliminate the original loopholes. The DISC tax provision is a good example. In 1971 the Congress, at the request of the President, enacted a proposal to allow United States firms selling overseas to set up domestic national sales corporations. This gave them special tax advantages for staying in the United States.

The new loophole, the DISC provision, does nothing about one of the root causes of the problem—the present special tax advantage given to the United States corporations that set up foreign subsidiaries, allowing them to defer taxes on the undistributed earnings of these subsidiaries. Secretary Connally contended that the new DISC law was necessary in order to make it "as attractive from a tax standpoint for United States companies to produce goods in the United States for export to world markets as it is for them to build their factories in foreign countries and produce abroad."

His statement amounted to the extraordinary contention—agreed to by the Congress—that we had to have a new tax loophole in order to correct the damage done by a loophole already in existence. It apparently never occurred to anyone to close the existing loophole—that is, take away the tax advantage for United States corporations forming foreign subsidiaries—and we may guess why: the giant corporations that benefit from the existing loopholes and export U.S. jobs would object.

Who loses from that kind of special tax action? Who else but the average taxpayer. In 1964 the median family income for a family of four was $7,488, and the tax in federal income and payroll deductions was $898—12 percent. In 1969 the median income for such a family, with inflated prices, had risen to around $9,500, and, despite much-heralded tax cuts, total federal taxes had risen for that family to $1,411—15 percent.

The result was that by mid-1972, when most United States taxpayers were being flattened by both higher prices and unfair taxes—including increased and regressive Social Security payroll taxes, not based on the ability of a worker to pay—corporate profits rose to a record annual rate of $93.1 billion.

Even *The Wall Street Journal* began to get uneasy. On the front page on August 2 was a report by Goldman, Sachs that "Federal tax cuts have helped corporations much more than individuals," and the story warned that, because of this, there was a "great risk" of more taxes.

A President who would take the lead could make a major difference. He could make a difference in income tax fairness and in securing enactment of stiff inheritance and estate tax rates.

But even with a President who is willing to make tax reform his major issue, tax action will still have to start with the people. And there are some signs that it is brewing.

Ex–Peace Corpsman Leonel Castillo was recently elected city comptroller in Houston. Operating from an office where the incumbent has generally been neither seen nor heard, he is churning up great waves of citizen response by announcing a "tax avoider of the week." Backed up by careful, mostly volunteer, research, he names a valuable building or property each week that is assessed at only a small fraction of its actual worth. And he makes clear that this means that other people are paying more than their share.

Linking up these kinds of efforts around the country and engendering others, a citizens' tax action movement could be the catalytic force to help return power and income to the people and take the rich off welfare.

CHAPTER

II

If a Little Capitalism Is Good, What's Wrong with a Lot?

For thirty years both the Republicans and the Democrats have agreed in general on how the country should be run. Both parties say that gross inequities in the economic system should be evened out somewhat. The government should fund programs and grant subsidies.

Whatever political debate there has been has skirted the real cause of the inequities. For the legislators, it's mostly been a matter of what program and how much subsidy—and to whom.

What's the result? After all the talk, the rich have only grown richer—the private ownership of capital, the means of production, has become more and more concentrated. Often, the devices nominally directed at correcting the balance have done just the opposite. Some subsidies are obvious and direct. Some are indirect. Many are hidden altogether.

The most secret and insidious subsidy is the one that

allows people to get rich from the misery and boredom of working people. Many jobs are highly dangerous. Many others are dreary and dull. One traditional liberal answer to this problem is for government to step in after the fact and attempt to provide some recompense to the working victims of this system. The New Populism calls for a change in the system itself.

Just how is the American system working? Here's one example. Walter Brown, aged forty, is a coke oven worker at the Clairton, Pennsylvania, plant of the U.S. Steel Corporation.

Mr. Brown wears wooden pallets under his shoes and a rubber mask for protection. He works all day on top of a battery of hot brick ovens, pulling off the heavy steel oven lids with a long iron bar and dumping in coal. As *The Wall Street Journal* has reported, his job

> is hot, filthy, monotonous and dangerous . . . surrounded by thick acrid smoke.
>
> The bricks he walks range in temperature up to 180°, and the steel lids up to 480°. Walls of flame from surrounding ovens shoot over his head. There is no roof; when it rains or snows, it rains or snows on Walter Brown.

Mr. Brown has worked at the mill for eighteen years, seven on this same job. He inhales tar, methane, benzine, hydrogen sulfide, carbon monoxide, coal dust, coke dust, and particles of pure carbon. He has headaches (no wonder!)—and he is ten times more likely to die of lung cancer than the average steel worker.

Walter Brown is only one of millions of American workers who suffer enormous daily hazards doing incredibly hard work to make the capitalistic system function and to make its owners richer.

The New Populism

He—and all of us—are on the receiving end of a kind of chamber-of-commerce ballyhoo that distorts the "work ethic" to justify this system and to keep it in being.

It is noteworthy that those who laud the virtues of this system loudest generally work in clean, safe, and attractive offices. President Nixon himself, praising the ennobling effect of work on those who perform it, once said that there's as much dignity in emptying bedpans as there is in serving as President of the United States. So far as is known, no emptier of bedpans has ever been heard to agree.

Walter Brown and millions of other American workers exemplify the "Hazard-Drudgery Compensation Ratio," as I call it, a relationship that is endemic in our society. If the hazard or drudgery of a job is high, compensation tends to be low. If the hazard or drudgery of a job is low, compensation tends to be high. It's another strange application of the work ethic. And it results from the fact that millions of workers are trapped in their economic class, are a captive work force.

The hazards are real. In 1970, official reports indicate that more than 14,000 employees were killed on the job, over 2 million were disabled, 8 million were injured, and nearly 400,000 contracted an industrial disease.

These figures are bad approximations, since industrial casualty rates are scaled down systematically. The industrial toll in human lives is probably two to three times higher than official figures indicate.

State and federal agencies have traditionally shown too little concern for the dangers of working. This is an attitude on their part that is greatly appreciated by the leaders of industry. Until 1963 the black lung disease of coal miners was not even officially recognized as a separate medical condition, and today, brown lung, a textile dust disease, is still not held to be a disease for which you

37

can claim compensation in most states. We are only now seriously beginning to study the dangers of asbestos, chemical gases such as chlorine and methane, radiation, and other such on-the-job hazards.

Not much news space is given to these killers and cripplers. We focus on the tragedies of war, on automobile deaths, and occasionally on major mine or industrial disasters. Too often, the only public attention given to the ordinary worker is in the form of carefully gathered statistics on strikes—the man-hours and production lost. In fact, the number of days lost because of work injuries in 1970 was ten times the total lost because of strikes or walkouts.

The natural aim of American business corporations today is to maximize profits. The health and safety of the worker are a secondary consideration at best. Corporation managers and owners concentrate on profits, and the American worker pays the hidden costs of death, disability, and injury.

The introduction of new machinery and new and more toxic materials has made the worker's job environment even worse. Improved safety and health precautions have not kept pace with industrial development. Under our system, corporate managers and owners have full responsibility for the plant, and they resist interference with job conditions—or even investigations. Management tends to see workers as things to be used to produce goods at as high a volume and as low a cost as is possible—until they wear out. Aside from the inhumanity of this system, its economic unsoundness and inefficiency is also lost on most owners and managers, and on a good many public officials as well.

But the system continues because those most hurt by it have the least power to change it. Economic power, translated into political power, enables business and industry to water down safety legislation before it can be passed and to weaken the enforcement of the health and safety laws that do manage to get on the books. The regulators and the regulated tend to come from the same nest. They go from industry to government enforcement agency and back again with comfortable regularity. The interests of industry tend to become intertwined with the interests of government.

Beginning in the late 1960s, the federal government started holding hearings on job health and safety. The leaders of industry trooped before Congress in droves. They seemed to be worried that safety laws would bring down whole industries. Some illiterate inspector, hired by the government, they said, might come back to a plant that had turned him down earlier for a job and "padlock your gates and have you fined $1,000 a day if you don't do as he says."

They argued that workers are responsible for their own lack of safety. They talked about "education" of the worker as the major need. They gently slapped themselves on the wrists for not "educating" as well as they should. The National Association of Manufacturers testified:

> In the last analysis, successful accident prevention depends on the effective motivation of the individual worker since human error is a causal factor in most industrial accidents. The development of this motivation depends on the development of effective communication between management and employee. This communication process cannot be improved by threats of civil or criminal sanctions against the employer.

With those arguments, backed up by enormous economic and political power, industry was able to get the proposed legislation watered down. Not satisfied with that, they went to work to weaken the law even further in its administration.

Consider the problem of noise. Even though other industrial countries have for years recognized that high noise levels not only can cause deafness but can be involved in heart disease, hormone imbalance, and other adverse physical effects, the United States lags behind. Our government does recognize that some noise standards must be set for jobs. Government officials initially proposed a standard of 85 decibels. General Motors and other companies opposed that standard. So the government backed down, and a compromise standard of 90 decibels was established—a noise standard that guarantees serious deafness for 15 to 20 percent of American workers.

And remember that chamber-of-commerce fear that the turned-down or discharged worker would reappear as an inspector? The government swallowed that argument, hook, line, and sinker. They decided that unionists or workers could not be inspectors under the law because only those who come from business management have the necessary experience to ensure *fair* enforcement.

But whether they come from the work force or from management, there are not many inspectors in any event —five hundred of them altogether and only fourteen industrial hygienists in the whole country to look after the health and safety of 55 million workers in over 4 million places of work.

Workers not only can't get an assurance of safety, they can't even get crucial information about the conditions they work in. Industry and government have worked together to ring down the "trade secret" curtain to prevent disclosure of the content of gases in the air workers breathe.

The New Populism

Once again, the traditional liberal trust that things will be better if good programs can be enacted has been distorted by those in power, in and out of government. To administer the health and safety legislation that has been passed in the last few years, President Nixon appointed George Guenther, a former hosiery company president. Six out of twelve members of the National Advisory Committee are from business, as are two of the remaining "public" members. The chairman of the committee is Howard Pyle, president of the National Safety Council, an organization known for its pro-industry bias.

Industry need not have been so worried about the new law. In the chemicals industry, complicated and dangerous new processes are being introduced at the rate of five to six hundred every year. After the new law went into effect, *Chemical Engineering* proudly ran an article by Secretary of Labor James D. Hodgson admitting that "there are numerous occupational hazards inherent in the business of the chemical process industries." But, he went on, "The new occupational safety and health law will not, in general, require any radical changes. It will merely require that those responsible improve upon the safety and health measures that are already applicable."

"I owe my soul to the company store," is an old song refrain—and it's a just complaint of many workers. The company doctor is no better than the store. This one professional group could do more than any other to improve working conditions, but unfortunately, in a majority of cases, the company doctor truly works for the company.

In most plants, the doctor will not allow the worker to see his own files. Many accidents and diseases are diagnosed wrongly to prevent company liability.

The American Medical Association parrots the industry myth of worker carelessness as the chief cause of industrial accidents and disease, and it has consistently urged that doctors report on accidents at work only if they see fit. And so black lung and brown lung (the textile worker's byssinosis) are regularly diagnosed and reported as emphysema or some other disease, and the doctors assume that lung cancers have no connection with the working environment.

Workers are left without compensation for disability or with inadequate compensation, and many die unnecessarily, never knowing that they were killed by the noxious environment of their workplace.

Dr. I. E. Buff of Charleston, West Virginia, is one of the conscientious doctors who are trying to change things. In 1970 he testified before a Senate committee:

> I went down there and I visited. And I slipped into three mills with the employees on the change of shift. I put on old clothes and made it appear I had tobacco in my mouth. . . . And I looked like a textile worker, as old as I am, because they have them my age. And I found something that most people don't know. It is hell in there. I have been in coal mines . . . but imagine being in a place where you can't see very far ahead of you, in a plant with no windows, supposed to be air-conditioned, and it is hot. You see lint everywhere. And you see no effort to control it.
>
> Then you go to ask doctors, "How about this byssinosis." White lung or cotton dust disease, and they don't want to even know about it and they don't even answer you sometimes. . . . This is an awful thing. The doctors will not chip the establishment. One doctor told me that if I said somebody had cotton dust disease, they would run me out of town. Another doctor says it would be unhealthy—

doctors of medicine. Sometimes I am wondering whether our oath of Hippocrates should not be restated the oath of Hypocrites because this makes me very, very angry because the people come first and not the physician or the industry.

In a Shell Oil Company insecticide plant in Denver, Colorado, a concerned doctor ran a series of tests on workers in the plant with the approval of the company. But when it became apparent that he was finding things wrong—like a connection between the workers' abnormal brain patterns and the noxious fumes in the plant— the employer kicked him out of the plant. In the hearing about the case before a Senate committee, a worker related the result:

The company didn't even want us to take the blood samples. . . . They didn't want us to talk to Metcalf [the doctor]. We can't get to Metcalf anymore. There is no way in the world that we can get to *him* to even talk to this man.

The same worker gave a good indication of the attitude of the company doctor:

Two or three weeks ago we had a man knocked out with chlorine, and we dragged him out, took him to the dispensary, and the doctor said no problem, he could go to work the next day. Well, he couldn't cough, breathe very well, and [the company doctor said] he was able to go back to work.

All of this illustrates one of the central weaknesses of the American system. The worker has no real power or control over his job. And it's just tough luck if he gets hurt. Eighteen million American workers are not even covered by workmen's compensation laws.

For those who are covered, compensation is administered by a state agency. And if a worker is going to get hurt, it's a whole lot better for him to get hurt in Arizona than anywhere else. In the rest of the states, the injured worker and his family have a hard time living. Most state laws provide for maximum total disability payments that are below the poverty level for a four-member family—often substantially below it.

In Oklahoma, for example, the family of a worker killed on the job receives only $13,500—not much payment for a man's life used up in industry. If the injured worker lives but is totally and permanently disabled, the maximum benefit he can get is only $60 a week, and, no matter how long he lives, the total payment cannot exceed $25,000. Medical care is limited to sixty days. There is no extra maintenance payment to help the worker live while trying to rehabilitate himself for another job.

But there are a lot of ways to kill or injure a person. Bad air and dangerous machines are the most obvious. You can also do it with jobs that turn workers into machines. Joe Glazer, who sings people's songs, says it all in "You Gotta Fight That Line." The last verse goes like this:

You gotta move, man, move like a super machine,
Gotta hustle, gotta rustle, it's a crazy scene.
Wanna scream, wanna holler, wanna call the cops—
But it don't help none, 'cause the line never stops.

Let me tell you what I've seen about the way management operates. I attended the 1972 stockholders meeting of General Motors. I was involved in the Project on Corporate Responsibility—the group that purchased stock in GM in order to try to initiate reforms from within, or at least to publicize the need for change. For openers, we proposed that a committee be set up to study breaking up this company, which now has 800,000 employees and more annual revenue than the gross national product of all but nine countries in the world. The idea was to divide this unwieldy and powerful monster into smaller units.

Of course, although the proposal was only for study, management voted proxies to defeat it by a margin of about 99 to 1. Other stockholder proposals were voted down by the same margin.

Then, by a vote of 99 to 1, management's single proposal, to increase incentive pay for top company officials by 25 percent, was adopted.

Richard Gerstenberg, chairman of GM, was already making—exclusive of investment income—a salary of $250,000, a yearly cash bonus of $250,000, and a yearly stock bonus worth $250,000. Big, round figures aren't hard to add up. He makes three-quarters of a million dollars every year.

As somebody noticed at the time, it's odd that a person making a base salary of $250,000 needs additional incentive to come to work. I found myself wondering what Mr. Gerstenberg would do if he didn't get his incentive, his half million in cash and stock bonuses—and the total was raised at the meeting. Would he call in sick a lot? Would he show up late for work too often? Would he take too long on coffee breaks?

Mr. Gerstenberg makes *ninety* times what the average worker on a GM assembly line makes. He also gets corporate jets, plush offices, country club memberships, and a company limousine—but in sheer cash GM's chairman makes ninety times more than the worker who slaps a door on a car every forty seconds, eight hours a day, five days a week, fifty weeks a year. The worker gets no share in skyrocketing auto profits, no special incentives—just a salary for a dull, dehumanizing job.

There is something wrong with the distribution of ownership and job control.

A good many corporate managers believe that factory workers are somehow different from other human beings —they must be unambitious and uncaring or they wouldn't be on the assembly line in the first place. GM's James Roche, when board chairman, put it this way: workers are people who "reject responsibility."

But Douglas Fraser of the United Auto Workers says it's just the opposite. "When a guy tells you the workers are not like you and me, that's nonsense," he says. "It's precisely because they are like you and me that the companies are having the goddamn problem. The workers are thinking, 'What the hell am I doing here?'"

The surprise would be if an assembly-line worker ever actually liked his job.

Studs Terkel recorded the conversation of a steel-worker in Chicago:

The day I get excited about my job is the day I go to a head shrinker. How are you gonna get excited about pulling steel? It's like slavery.

Picasso can point to a painting. I think I've worked harder than Picasso, and what can I point to? A writer can point to a book. Everybody should have something to point to.

If a carpenter built a cabin for poets, I think the least the poets owe the carpenter is just three or four one-liners on the wall. A little plaque: "Though we labor with our minds, this place we can relax in was built by someone who can work with his hands. And his work is as noble as ours." . . . I think the poet owes something to the guy who builds the cabin for him.

Workers' dissatisfaction with their jobs and their job lives came to a head at GM's Vega plant at Lordstown, Ohio, in 1972. The assembly line in that plant—built to be the world's fastest and most highly automated—carried 101 cars past each worker every hour. Each worker had 36 seconds to perform his assigned task. Not satisfied with this speeded-up pace, management fired more than five hundred workers at the plant and divided up their tasks among the remaining workers.

And it's not just at Lordstown. What about the auto industry as a whole? The car plants are plagued with absenteeism that runs as high as 12 percent on Saturdays, for example, in spite of time-and-a-half pay on that day. Absenteeism, generally, has increased by as much as 100 percent in the last ten years.

A lot of new workers were recruited for the new plant at Lordstown. The average age is twenty-four. They did not like being treated on the same level as the automobile parts they handled. So, when the Lordstown line was speeded up, they voted overwhelmingly to strike.

"The job pays good, but it's driving me crazy," a Lordstown worker told Barbara Garson, as she reported in *Harper's.* That's typical of the views of most industrial workers. The plain truth is that many people are bored to death with their jobs. And white-collar workers, where jobs often consist of one piece of trivia piled on another, are just as dissatisfied as assembly-line workers.

What does a worker want from a job? A University of Michigan survey showed that good pay ranks *fifth*. The 1,500 workers interviewed gave higher value to: interesting work; enough help and equipment to get the job done; enough information to get the job done; and enough authority to do the job. The opportunity to develop special abilities was ranked sixth.

Workers want to be treated as thinking, feeling, mature adults. Instead, they are treated like children. Management thinks they must be controlled, disciplined, and made to follow precise instructions to the letter. It presently takes a new automobile worker only thirty minutes to learn his job.

A member of the National Management Association expressed the typical management view when he said, "In general 'job enrichment' entails a stimulation of some intellectual need and fulfillment of that need. That fulfillment involves a thought process which in turn involves decision-making and personal responsibility; both of which will be and are avoided by the average hourly worker."

That is the American view. But it isn't the view of management in some other countries now providing worrisome competition to American manufacturers. The Japanese, for example, give workers access to decision-making processes concerning their work, creating a teamwork atmosphere in the plant—although this may have begun to break down some.

The Saab and Volvo automobile companies in Sweden allow small teams of workers to produce an entire finished automobile. Jobs are rotated, and the groups are allowed to set their own schedules, devise their own work methods, and train their own assistants. Volvo pays the small groups an extra fee for training new workers. Workers are involved in decision-making on quality control, material handling, tool changes, and rate of work. The programs are voluntary, and pay is based on productivity.

In this country, management's view has been that work is either "thinking" work or "sweating" work. Bosses boss and workers work. And never the twain shall meet. Jobs continue to be deadly dull and deadly in fact because workers do not share in job control, because they do not share in the "bossing" as well as in the "sweating."

Some companies have begun to change. More will have to, as younger workers, not so tied to their jobs as their fathers were, come into the work force. Motorola is experimenting with replacing the assembly line. Parker Pen long ago adopted a plan, originated by Joe Scanlon, which attempts to reduce the sweating work and to get all of the workers involved in the thinking work as well. It has been highly successful at Parker; production has increased. Under the plan the workers share in the profits, and that is a vital point.

As Suzannah Lessard has written in the *Washington Monthly,* job enrichment alone is not enough. "Reorganizing an auto plant so that workers get to put a whole Vega together rather than turn identical bolts all day long isn't going to make their job appealing—particularly after they have put the ten thousandth Vega together—only tolerable." Terkel's steelworker wondered how Michelangelo would have felt if he had to create the Sistine Chapel a thousand times a year: "Don't you think that would dull even Michelangelo's mind?"

Let's go a step further. Some of the "sweat" jobs ought to be eliminated altogether. When the number of the worst jobs in our society has been reduced to as few as possible, perhaps all of us should have to share in the remaining ones. But it's even more important that people get a better share of the fruits of their work. "The very least measure which could make a dent in the fundamental unfairness would be to give the auto worker a piece of the Vega and the garbageman a share in the company, a measure which would not be revolutionary, only economically just," writes Ms. Lessard.

Indeed, it's not a revolutionary idea. It's a rather old one. "To secure to each laborer the whole product of his labor, or as nearly as possible, is a worthy subject of any good government," Abraham Lincoln said.

Workers get caught in what I call the "Responsibility Catch"—the Catch-22 of sharing in ownership and job control. Here's how this particular piece of circular reasoning works out: management shares in ownership and is paid more and workers do not share in ownership and are paid less because, management says, workers have less responsibility. And yet workers cannot share in responsibility because, says management, that is the exclusive province of management.

Some American companies have fairly good profit-sharing plans; others have plans that are just another form of exploitation of labor. Sears, Roebuck has had a good profit-sharing plan since 1916. This plan has been a vital factor in attracting and keeping good employees and fostering a spirit of company teamwork. But there is a drawback to the Sears plan—it involves no sharing in responsibility by workers, no sharing in job control.

If profit without responsibility is bad, the converse is worse—that is, to ask workers to share in responsibility without sharing in profits is manifestly exploitative and unfair.

Responsibility-sharing and profit-sharing go together, and the way they can be assured is by sharing in ownership. One kind of worker, the "thinking" worker—management—gets stock bonuses and special stock purchase opportunities. What's wrong with that system for the rest of the workers?

A few people with some power have begun to say workers should participate in ownership. The experience of the Pillsbury family shows what's beginning to happen. Wealthy, fifty-year-old George Pillsbury found to his astonishment that when he retired from business to manage his family's investments his rate of accumulating wealth accelerated. A Harris survey has reported that 68 percent of Americans now agree that the rich get richer and the poor get poorer, and George Pillsbury says, "The fact of the matter is it's true."

George Pillsbury is a Nixon conservative. His son, Charles, twenty-four, is a McGovern liberal. But they both agree that it is essential to "slow this irrational accumulation of wealth by the wealthy, and to allow those who have nothing—who have no property at all— to gain access to capital, to income-producing property." They advocate a plan by which workers can gain ownership in the company they work for.

Former Governor Luis A. Ferré of Puerto Rico subscribes to the same views—and, like the Pillsburys, he has been influenced by Louis Kelso's *Two Factor Theory: The Economics of Reality*, which proposes a plan for ownership-sharing. Governor Ferré set up a new program in Puerto Rico by which Puerto Rican workers could share in the ownership of corporations that do business there.

Meanwhile, elsewhere, no real progress is being made toward democratizing the workplace, and the steps being taken toward job enrichment, health, and safety are small and halting.

Are there any other obvious solutions to the problem? Classical socialism would abolish private ownership and vest it in the state. But, where practiced, this can result in workers trading one set of economic bosses for another set of equally repressive political bosses.

Nor can the workers hope to appeal to the corporate conscience. That is not the nature of the beast. The law says a corporation is a "person," but saying this doesn't make it so. Corporations are not people, nor do they usually exhibit what we think of as the higher human traits. Their natural motivation is very narrow: they serve the interests of those who own and manage them. So workers have to plug into this natural force.

What about the unions? They are no final answer. First of all, the majority of American workers are not unionized. But even where workers are represented by unions, the record concerning job control and ownership is not exemplary.

In the field of job health and safety, the Oil, Chemical and Atomic Workers Union has been very active, but this is a conspicuous exception. In the past, unions have tended to relegate health and safety issues to the bottom of the list for negotiations. Some of them may have swallowed the management argument that safety precautions cut down profits and thus cut down on wage increases and jobs.

There are ways by which union leaders actually work with owners against safety. The former leaders of the United Mine Workers were notorious for connivance with mine owners to neglect safety standards. The price of this was the death and disability of thousands of miners.

Many international unions have safety divisions that can only be described as skeletal. The International Brotherhood of Teamsters, with a membership of approximately two million, has no safety division at all. Many union locals have no research available on the subject when they are facing tough contract negotiations concerning health and safety. Sometimes a job safety committee is set up, half union and half management. But most of these committees, which usually meet at the whim of management and under the threat of management's veto, are less than effective.

Pressure from union members is mounting on the

health and safety issues. A lot of younger members, particularly, have begun to recognize that things do not
have to remain the way they've always been. Also, union
locals are becoming more aggressive. The steelworkers'
local of the Wheeling-Pittsburgh Steel Corporation now
has a contract that allows them to walk off the job and
receive unemployment compensation when health and
safety conditions get bad enough.

Unions have been particularly slow to push for job
enrichment and the right of the worker to share in job
control. These are not issues where there has been much
hard bargaining. One reason for this is the union feeling
that they can negotiate only on a few demands—more
members, it is said, want increased wages and fringe
benefits than want job improvement. But worker surveys
are increasingly showing that this is an incorrect assump-
tion. Unions will have to respond.

Actually, most union leaders probably don't want
workers to share in ownership. They worry that the fundamental labor-management confrontation will be
fuzzed up, that bargaining will become more complex,
and that ultimately unions will be destroyed.

There is no reason why the last fear should be true.
Collective bargaining will still be a necessity, even when
union workers own a part of the industry. Unorganized
workers will still lack the group power necessary to assure their rights. While the other fears are probably appropriate—labor relations and bargaining will become
more complex—why should that worry us? For that matter, why should it bother union leaders? Ownership is
power, and a share in ownership for workers will give
them a share in power. Workers will benefit by being able
to use their increased power to effect better working
conditions and to get a fair share in the fruits of their
labor.

Indications exist that consumers would also benefit. Parker Pen Company's Scanlon plan, where workers share in both management responsibility and profits, has maintained productivity at such a rate that the company has been able to keep the price of its ballpoint pen at $1.98, established in 1955. Too, if workers shared in ownership, inflationary wage demands would become more subject to natural pressures in the economy—as opposed to government-imposed pressures.

And, probably, there would be an improvement in the quality of the goods produced. A former employee of mine who once worked on an automobile assembly line told me about the anger and frustration he had to live with there. "My job was to put in the transmission grease and then screw in a plug on every car that came by. The same thing, hour after hour, all day long. Put in the transmission grease and screw in the plug.

"Sometimes they would speed up the line to get out the production they wanted, faster, so that they could shut down and lay us off quicker. I tell you the truth, Senator, and I'm not proud of it, some days I wouldn't be able to get the transmission grease in more than two-thirds of the cars that went by. I'd just go ahead and screw in the plug anyway and try to catch up on the next one."

Unions are more and more going to have to respond to men who feel like this, to the rising anger and frustration of the American workers whom they represent. Too many union members are beginning to feel the way Terkel's steelworker does: "I think that what happened was the people who organized the working men forgot the spirit and paid more attention to the organization. They became as corporate as the corporations they were fighting."

If workers are to share in job control and ownership,

government action is required. And it cannot be left to the individual states. One state can now charter a corporation to operate throughout the whole country. Most state laws governing corporations are very lax, and corporations seek out the state with the loosest laws.

The New Populist response to this sloppy and dangerous situation is very simple: interstate corporations should be federally chartered. And the charter should include a kind of Bill of Rights for workers—and consumers and stockholders too. One of those worker rights should be sharing in ownership and job control.

And this right could and should be self-executing. Any worker could go to court—for himself and others—to enforce the law.

By this means, and by instituting worker democracy in its own offices, the government should intervene to complement the best aspects of the natural forces at work in our job society, rather than to accept these forces and try to compensate for their worst aspects. Treat the cause—concentrated ownership and the workers' need to share in control of their jobs—rather than just the symptoms.

After all, as Charles Pillsbury says, "If capitalism is good for a few, then it's good for everyone."

CHAPTER

III

Buttons Say "Free" This Person or "Free" That Person: What About "Free Enterprise"?

When I was in Hungary in the spring of 1971, I spent a good deal of time learning about its foreign and domestic economic policies. I particularly wanted to know about the new directions that were being charted.

I talked at some length with the prime minister, the head of the central bank, and the foremost academic economist. They explained the New Economic Mechanism then being instituted. They told how the government had moved to secure wide discussion within political and economic circles of how the new policy should work.

As in the Soviet Union and other Eastern European countries, the Hungarians recognize that industry and agriculture must be modernized rapidly to satisfy the increasingly insistent demands for consumer goods and to earn foreign exchange.

Before 1971 the totally planned Hungarian economy

was running into considerable trouble. Technological advances were slow. Economic distortions occurred because, it was felt, no person or group of persons was able always to decide efficiently and wisely about what goods ought to be produced and in what quantity—whether to produce more shoes, say, or more raincoats—and how to price the goods that were produced. With a totally planned economy, it was impossible to keep all the workers employed efficiently.

"I went with a party official to visit one of our better manufacturing enterprises," one government official told me in Budapest. "It was a plant that employed a large number of people, and I asked the plant manager how many workers he could discharge and still operate efficiently, if there was no counterpressure from the government or the party. He said that he could operate efficiently with 10 percent fewer workers. And that is one of our more efficient enterprises; most of our enterprises have what we call 'in-plant' unemployment of 15 percent: that is, they employ an average of 15 percent more workers than they actually need."

The New Economic Mechanism in Hungary calls for letting the market have greater control over the nature, quantity, and price of goods that will be produced and the question of where people will work. The government still intends to control the prices of imported goods, agricultural products, and natural resources, but it has already begun to relax controls elsewhere in the economy. The Hungarian officials were most concerned about the surplus workers, and some officials felt that the new policy had been too cautious in this regard; no progress had been made on the problem at the time I was there.

I was struck by two aspects of the New Economic Mechanism: one is the movement in the direction of greater reliance upon the market, rather than total government planning. The other is the large number of government and academic experts who are involved in discussing, revising, debating, and deciding what kind of economic management system Hungary should have. These people are trying to see how the heavy lid of control can be raised somewhat without bringing on intolerable inflation and unacceptable unemployment.

All this is taking place in Hungary, in the very shadow of Soviet force—the march on Czechoslovakia in 1968 shows that the Soviets are sensitive to revisionism in Eastern Europe—and despite the rigid constraints of traditional Marxist-Leninist dogma.

In our own country there is no fear of invasion, nor are we bound to stay within an unchangeable dogmatic framework. Yet we have begun to change our economic management system radically with almost no public debate or discussion of alternatives, and with no comparable involvement of large numbers of our people in making the new policy.

President Nixon has launched us upon a radically different kind of economic management system from what we have ever had before. We will never again be the same. No American government will ever again be able to stand aside from the path of oncoming inflation and unemployment. Few know that there was, and is, an alternative to increased government control when inflation and unemployment are the problem, as they were in the summer of 1971.

Why not try a little really free enterprise? It cannot be worse than what we have. Some of the socialist countries are taking steps in that direction. Why shouldn't we? Despite imposed government controls, prices in the United States have continued unacceptably high, and the number of people without jobs has remained tragically large, in a country where there are plenty of things that need to be done.

In 1972 I went down to the Sheraton Park Hotel in Washington, D.C., to look over the conference on "Industry and the Future." The meeting had attracted many industrialists and big businessmen. It was a kind of festival of self-congratulation for American business. And, in spite of the more than modest means of the participants, it was the taxpayers who financed this celebration through funds from tax-exempt foundations and direct federal grants.

The conference discussed the future impact and nature of technological developments, along with environmental questions and nearly everything else—except President Nixon's economic controls, which the conferees largely supported. Where, I wondered, were the traditional defenders of free enterprise? Doesn't it seem strange, I asked myself, that either they are quiet or docile in the face of greater government controls or they even speak out in support of controls?

Then, I reflected, it's not so strange. If you have the power and can pretty much control the government, you don't mind government control.

I had long felt that Keynesian economics, as practiced by the United States government in the last several years, didn't work out right. The Keynesian principles involve two main factors. First, there is the manipulation of *monetary* policy—that is, increasing the supply of money to stimulate economic growth, or tightening the money supply to retard economic growth. And then there is the manipulation of *fiscal* policy—that is, increasing government expenditures and reducing taxes to speed economic growth, or decreasing government expenditures and increasing taxes to slow economic growth.

Objective evidence convinced me that these kinds of

macroeconomic, nationwide economic tools, might change nationwide statistics, but that the conditions they were supposed to affect were not always nationwide. Some industries had such power in the money market that they could still soak up a disproportionate share of the available money, even when a lid was put on the money supply and interest rates were raised, while other industries, notably housing, with less power in the money market, were disastrously affected by tight money and high interest rates.

Also, I discovered that inflationary wage and price increases—along with idle plant capacity and unemployment—could not always be expressed in some uniform set of national figures. These factors varied from industry to industry.

Most of all, my moral sense was offended by the conventional notion that there always had to be a trade-off between inflation and unemployment. True, there always had been a choice like this. The economy had always been a sort of seesaw: as unemployment went up on one end, inflation went down on the other; as inflation went up, unemployment went down. It didn't seem right.

Early in President Nixon's Administration, I was one of those who criticized the policies the government was then following—economist John Kenneth Galbraith of Harvard was another. I said it was "heartless and indefensible" to tighten up the money supply and decrease the fiscal stimulus in order, deliberately, to induce economic recession—in effect throwing millions of people out of work so as to bring down the rate of inflation.

Professor Galbraith and I, and others, advocated government intervention in wage, price, and related decisions in preference to the intolerably high rate of unemployment. I called for strictly limited intervention. I wanted to see permanent government machinery set up for the institution of voluntary wage, price, and other guidelines. The new agency would have the power to enforce selective and temporary freezes, where necessary, to keep such increases within acceptable limits.

At first President Nixon was adamantly opposed to *any* kind of wage and price restraints. Then, when it became obvious that his monetary and fiscal policies were not working, he switched abruptly.

But, when he switched, he swallowed the whole camel. He embraced Lord Keynes as if they were going steady. A President who wouldn't intervene at all suddenly intervened totally. Professor James Tobin said, "Never before in peacetime [*sic*] has an American government subjected virtually every price and wage in the country to legally enforceable ceilings."

The result is a weird alignment: people like President Nixon and the leaders of the U.S. Chamber of Commerce are on one side; and people like Ralph Nader and myself are on the other. This alignment illustrates the choices in economic management that will be made by America in the 1970s. It also points up the debate that is going to grow more and more heated within the traditional liberal camp.

Professor Galbraith and I debated these choices before Ralph Nader's Symposium on Corporate Responsibility in Washington in the early part of 1972.

We agreed that a proper goal of government should be better distribution of wealth and income, but we disagreed absolutely how to bring it about.

Professor Galbraith and President Nixon believe that bigness is both inevitable and, probably, benign. It's just a matter of who owns and controls the big companies.

Professor Galbraith believes in the classic socialism of public ownership, under which General Motors would continue to be as big as it is but would be owned and controlled by the government. President Nixon believes in the present kind of corporate socialism, which is much like the Zaibatsu system that existed in Japan prior to World War II. Under this system General Motors would continue to be as big as it is but would, in effect, own and control the government.

The New Populism disagrees with both. It holds that bigness is generally bad and tends to grind down individuals, whether the concentrated power is exercised by the government or by corporations.

The fact is that bigness is not more efficient. Belief in bigness aided Lockheed and the Penn Central in becoming huge and powerful complexes. But as things came out, they would have long since gone down the drain owing to inefficiency, except that they were able to get the government to bail them out.

I doubt that any person or government commission is smart enough to decide in advance what goods ought to be produced at what price and in what quantity, or where people ought to work and at what wage. The market is a better planning mechanism.

There are natural market forces that can help hold down prices and unemployment. The government must step in where these forces do not work and hold them within acceptable bounds, but our government increasingly has intervened *against* natural market pressures.

Few of us realize just how bad economic concentration is in America, or that it is far worse than it has ever been.

In 1947, at the end of World War II, the top 200 industrial corporations accounted for 45 percent of all manufacturing in the United States. What happened after that would show up dramatically on a graph indicating the number of mergers in this century—that is, where two or more companies combine into one company, thereby concentrating their economic power.

The New Populism

The chart would show a kind of Pikes Peak of mergers just before President Theodore Roosevelt took office. Then they drop back down. Just before Franklin Roosevelt took office, mergers rise on the chart to a kind of Mount Everest point. Then they go back down again. From 1960 on—through the Kennedy, Johnson, and Nixon administrations—the merger line goes up, up, up —and off the chart!

Acquisitions of one corporation by another from 1947 to 1968 totaled more than $50 billion in corporate assets —more than $15 billion in 1968 alone. Thus, by 1968, the top 200 industrial corporations—that is, a tiny fraction of 1 percent of the approximately 186,000 manufacturing corporations in the United States—had so increased their size and share of the market that they controlled more than 60 percent of all United States manufacturing. They accounted for slightly over 30 percent of total income in the whole country.

These huge manufacturing corporations wield enormous economic power over the rest of our economy— the nonmanufacturing sectors, particularly wholesale and retail trade. Industrial organization economists divide production markets into 400 separate "industries," ranging from razor blades and breakfast cereals to steel and automobiles. They divide these 400 industries into a competitive group and a noncompetitive group. Where the four largest firms in an industry account for under 40 percent of the industry's total sales, the industry is classed as one that is effectively competitive.

But as the share of the market controlled by the four largest firms in an industry moves into the 40 to 50 percent range, the industry starts to lose more and more of its competitive character and takes on more and more of the behavior patterns and performance features of a monopolized industry.

When the figure passes 50 percent, when four or fewer firms in an industry control 50 percent or more of the market, the industry becomes a "shared monopoly." Market forces are so muted at this point that there is little hope for the consumer to buy at competitive prices—and there are other unwholesome results as well.

Dr. William G. Shepherd has documented that one-half of the total manufacturing industries in America in 1966, or 200 of them, accounting for nearly two-thirds of all manufactured goods produced in the United States, fall into the noncompetitive category.

And in the still higher range of concentration, about one-third of all U.S. manufacturing output was produced in 1966 by industries in which the four largest firms accounted for 70 percent or more of the industry's total sales.

Professor Shepherd documented similar patterns in the nonmanufacturing sectors of the United States economy, concluding:

> All in all at least 35 to 40 percent of market activity in the United States appears to take place under conditions of substantial market (monopoly) power.

Such monopoly power prevails, for example, in the steel, tire, automobile, aluminum, soap, container, and farm machinery industries. As of 1968, Campbell's Soup accounted for 90 percent of all soup manufactured in the United States. That is some kind of a system, but it's damn sure not the free enterprise system.

It is a system of concentrated economic power. And it has alarmingly serious economic and political consequences.

Shared monopolies set prices. The automobile industry is a prime example. The big three automobile compa-

nies—GM, Ford, and Chrysler—control 97 percent of
the domestic market for American-made cars, with GM
alone controlling over 54 percent. Even when foreign
imports are added in, the three biggest American companies still dominate the market with 83 percent of the
business.

The Nader Report on antitrust enforcement gives a
case study of how prices are set:

> In September 1956, Ford announced suggested
> price increases, ranging from $1 to $104; two weeks
> later GM announced new Chevrolet prices $50 to
> $166 higher than the year before; one week later
> Ford revised its prices upward, so that on ten mod-
> els the differences with Chevy were $1 or $2, while
> on two other models they were $10 to $11.

That's the way it works. Steel is another industry dominated by a shared monopoly. During 1970 and 1971
steel sales went down. Adam Smith, who wrote of the law
of supply and demand, might have been surprised to see
what happened. As demand for steel went down, steel
prices should have come down too. Not at all. Steel
prices went *up*. The steel companies, despite idle plant
capacity and heavy unemployment, increased unit prices
to make up for lost sales volume. The steel companies
were able to do this because they are not competitive.
They are more powerful than market pressures.

The ability to set prices in an industry, the lack of
competition, results in "unsatisfactory market performance: inflated selling costs, product imitation, higher-
than-competitive prices, collusive suppression of technological innovation, and persistently high rates of
return," as the *Yale Law Journal* has characterized the
automobile industry.

Shared monopolies can pass along the high costs of lax management and inefficiency. The consumer pays for lush offices, corporate jets, and extremely high management salaries. The head of ITT, Harold Geneen, for example, gets $812,000 per year.

Shared monopolies use large advertising expenditures to drive out smaller competitors and then to control the market. And the consumer pays. Dr. Frederic M. Scherer shows how at least a fourth of the $20 billion per year spent on advertising in the United States goes to buy "messages which serve little function but to mislead the consumer or cancel out rival messages."

Another $5 billion, he says, is wasted on "disfunctionally elaborate packaging," deceptive give-away programs, "accelerated styling changes which do nothing more than render last year's model obsolete," and similar noncompetitive promotional practices. The automobile industry's practice of changing car styles each year adds an average of $700 to the price of every car sold.

Inflated prices, caused by lack of competition, cost consumers $50 billion a year—5 percent of national income. Senator Philip Hart's Antimonopoly Subcommittee has said that prices in America would come down by as much as 20 percent if there were real competition in American industry.

Too high pricing by shared monopolies redistributes income and wealth in the wrong direction. Professor Shepherd found that of total, after tax, *manufacturing* corporation profits of $48 billion in 1967, 10 percent—$4.9 billion—represented extra monopoly profits over and above what would have been earned in the absence of excessive concentration.

He points out that between 1946 and 1967 the automobile industry, for example, earned nearly 17 percent on net worth, at a time when the average for all manufacturing corporations was just over 9 percent. That adds up to a redistribution of income of up to $500 million a year—coming out of ten million car buyers' pockets and going into the accounts of the relatively few stockholders in auto companies who control most of the stock.

For the whole economy, Professor Shepherd has estimated that shared monopolies redistribute to themselves and away from consumers $8.1 billion a year in monopoly profits. The "exclusive dealer" distribution system in the gasoline industry adds, according to Dr. Joe S. Bain of Berkeley, as much as four cents a gallon to what the consumer pays and thereby redistributes more than $3 billion in increased revenue—resulting in excessive profits—to the big oil corporations.

Concentrated economic power means that the small 2 percent of Americans who own 80 percent of all individually held corporate stock and 90 percent of all individually held corporate bonds get richer each year in income and wealth, at the expense of 98 percent of the people.

Workers lose because shared monopolies have increasingly priced American products out of the market. In effect, jobs are exported. Japanese workers make more Datsuns and Toyotas. Fewer workers are needed to make Chevrolets and Fords.

Consumers and workers lose in another way because of the lack of competition in American industry. Technological innovation lags or is suppressed. In the automobile industry, as economist Gardiner Means has pointed out, "if a new technique must promise a sixteen to twenty percent return on capital before it is substituted for the old, it will not be introduced." Excessive profits thus discourage innovation in the automobile industry, which waited fifteen years, for example, to meet the competition of small foreign cars. Even a former Ford vice-president, Donald Frey, will say that "the automatic transmission was the last major innovation of the industry." And that was developed in the 1930s.

In the steel industry Ralph Nader has shown that of thirteen major inventions between 1940 and 1955, none was developed by American steel companies. Most came from small European steel companies or individual inventors.

Noncompetitive American industry has not kept up with new techniques, and it has not kept up with the times. Consumers lose in product quality. Workers lose in exported jobs.

Even the American Management Institute agrees that bigness is bad in one major monopoly industry: "One cannot study General Motors' massive operation without experiencing an inescapable feeling—General Motors is too big. It is too big for the good of American businessmen who must deal with it and too big for the good of the country."

Franklin Roosevelt warned in 1938 that big business collectivism encourages an ultimate collectivism in government. The power of the few to manage the economic life of the nation, he said, must be diffused or it must ultimately be controlled. In 1971 President Nixon instituted wage and price controls. He did not intervene in the marketplace to make it work. He intervened to compensate for the symptoms that showed it was not working —simultaneous inflation and unemployment. Pricing power ostensibly moved from the corporate suites into government offices.

The government began to decide which industries could raise prices and which could not. It determined which workers deserved wage increases and which did not. Teachers were denied wage increases, but insurance companies were allowed to raise their premiums.

And it did not work. By mid-1972, prices were still too high, unemployment was still at 5.6 percent, and corporate profits were rising at the unprecedented annual rate of $93.1 billion.

The President had instituted wage and price controls —and he and the Congress had extended them—despite mountains of evidence that what was most needed was an effort to make the free enterprise system work.

The President began by believing in the trade-off between inflation and unemployment. So he had shut down on the spigots of monetary and fiscal stimulus, raising unemployment and bringing about, as economist Walter Heller said, "the first synthetic and purposely created recession in our history." But when the unemployment end of the seesaw went up, the inflation end did not go down. Arthur Burns conceded that "the rules of economics are not working quite the way they used to. . . . The traditional monetary and fiscal remedies cannot solve the problems of inflation and unemployment as quickly as national interest demands."

The planners were fighting the wrong cause. The problem was not too much demand; 27 percent of plant capacity was idle from 1969 through 1971. The President's own Council of Economic Advisers had pointed out in its 1971 report that there are two explanations usually given for the stubborn nature of inflation in the United States. "One relates the persistence of the inflation, after corrective measures have been taken, to the duration and magnitude of the preceding inflationary boom," they said. "The other traces the cause of structural changes in the economic system, especially but not exclusively connected with the concentration of economic power."

They and the government then proceeded to forget

the second explanation and acted entirely upon the first. In doing so, they ignored, too, a 1969 report of the President's own Cabinet Committee on Price Stability, which found that there was a "critical link" between inflation and concentrated market power, citing the steel industry as a case in point. "Between 1953 and 1959 steel was primarily responsible for the increase in the wholesale price index," the report stated. "Finished steel prices rose by 36% during the period, whereas all wholesale prices rose an average of 8.5%. Wholesale prices, exclusive of all metals and metals manufacturers, rose only 1.5% in the period."

This report to the President corroborated earlier studies that showed, for example, that during the 1950s the steel industry alone had been responsible for 40 percent of all inflation during that period and that the automobile industry, by itself, was responsible for nearly 20 percent.

Incredibly, the government, after these findings, not only instituted wage and price controls across the board and did nothing to stimulate competition, but it also proceeded to grant price increases for steel and automobiles.

In late 1971 American steel was dangerously overpriced, and the industry was under pressure from foreign imports. Plants were operating at about 50 percent of capacity. The last thing one would have thought that this industry and its 100,000 laid-off workers needed was a price increase. Yet that's just what they got.

The steel companies were allowed an across-the-board price increase of 3.6 percent, which each company could allocate to individual product lines as it wished. What happened thereafter gives more than a clue to the principal cause of our economic troubles. Virtually the entire increase in steel prices went into product lines in which the companies faced little foreign competition. Prices for cold-rolled steel, used in making cars and refrigerators and other appliances, went up 7.2 percent, double the across-the-board rate approved. Prices for structural steel, used in bridge and building construction, didn't go up at all.

There is still competition from foreign structural steel, and that competition held down the price. Where the steel companies had controlling market power, prices went up.

As if this weren't enough, the government took two other steps to keep the market from working. National Steel, the fourth-largest steel company in America, wanted to merge with Granite City, the twelfth-largest. "Don't mind us," the government said, "go right ahead." The new company is now the third-largest, and there is even less competition in what was already a noncompetitive, shared monopoly industry.

But what about foreign competition? The consumer lost again. This last safety valve is being choked off because the government has allowed the steel companies to run their own foreign policy and negotiate limits on steel coming in from foreign countries.

Prior to the institution of wage and price controls, the President's Cabinet Committee on Price Stability also announced its findings in regard to wages. It found a close relationship between high profits in highly concentrated industries and the pressure for wage increases in those same industries. "Recent research studies," the committee found, "show that wage rate increases are related to the level of profits and to increases in profits. Moreover, incomes of non-union employees, particularly the salaries and bonuses of management personnel, are likely to be higher in such firms than in those earning lower profits." (The committee also discovered that, even after paying higher wages, salaries, and bonuses, profits in the highly concentrated industries tended to be 50 percent higher than in moderately concentrated industries.)

Professor Scherer agrees. He says that because these concentrated industries are able to pass along excessive costs and earn excessive profits, they are vulnerable to wage demands rationalized on the basis of ability to pay. This vulnerability makes waves throughout the rest of the economy. "Once substantial wage increases have been won in key [concentrated] industries and the prices of industry products have risen," he states, "inflationary pressures spread as other unions attempt to emulate the initial example and as all employee groups try to compensate for increased costs of living by demanding still higher incomes."

President Nixon's wage and price controls didn't work. In the first place, the program might at least have been neat. Instead, it was the worst possible bureaucratic maze. There was a Pay Board and a separate Price Commission. There was a Cost of Living Council and separate advisory panels on health costs and interest and dividends. There was a Productivity Commission and something called an Inflation Alert that the Council of Economic Advisers was supposed to administer. And the Secretary of the Treasury and the Office of Management and Budget were in there somewhere. Most of them operated in private.

With across-the-board wage and price controls, the government was not only fighting a large snake with a rake when it needed a hoe, it was fighting with a short-handled rake at that. When we had controls during World War II, our Gross National Product was only one-fifth what it is today, and the total labor force was only 60 million, compared with today's 85 million. Even so, thirty years ago it took 60,000 paid employees, 250,000 full-time volunteers, 9 regional offices, 105 district offices, and 5,400 local price and rationing boards to administer wage and price controls. We don't have a fraction of that now—and I hope we never do again.

There's no need for across-the-board controls if we will restore competition to its professed importance in our economic system. Chester Bowles, who was head of OPA in World War II, has correctly described what is needed: "First, the immediate imposition of mandatory wage-price controls in the most concentrated sectors of industry (most of which, are, in effect, already operating outside the market system), and, second, the vigorous use of antitrust policy to help promote competitive behavior to a point where wage-price controls can be relaxed on an industry-by-industry basis."

Monopolies have ostensibly been illegal since 1890, and, under the Bowles system, when an industry quit violating the law, it would cease to be subject to controls. Each industry would carry in its pocket the key to its own release.

Even temporary controls would not have to be widespread. Just one-fourth of the industries fall into the heavily concentrated group. Only twenty-one major manufacturing industries with substantial monopoly power account for nearly one-third of all U.S. manufacturing. Five industries alone—steel, automobiles, telephone equipment, computers, and drugs—are responsible for at least $6 billion of unnecessary monopoly costs each year.

In 1972 the Federal Trade Commission decided, in one industry, to try to do something about economic concentration itself, rather than just to recommend alleviation of its adverse effects. The commission said that the breakfast cereal industry in America is a shared monopoly—that four companies, General Foods, General Mills, Kellogg's, and Quaker, control more than 70 percent of the breakfast cereal market. The commission found that these four companies had secured and maintained market control through excessive advertising, that their prices were 15 percent too high, and that the nutritional content of their products was deficient.

The commission did not recommend more rigid price controls on the products of these industries. It did not suggest government-imposed limits on their advertising budgets. Nor did it ask for stiffer laws on minimum nutritional content. The commission did not suggest more attractive government loans for the smaller cereal companies going out of business or increased assistance for their unemployed workers.

Instead, in a landmark decision, the Federal Trade Commission said that the root cause of unwholesome effects in the breakfast cereal industry was lack of competition, due to shared-monopoly market power. The commission announced that it was going into court to seek an order breaking up the big four cereal companies—all in violation of present antitrust laws—into a number of smaller, competitive companies. Each company would no longer have the economic power to set prices and each would have to vie with the others, through better prices and better products, for its share of the market.

What the Federal Trade Commission has done in regard to cereals can be done in the other shared-monopoly industries. Professor Walter Adams has said, "U.S. Steel is nothing more than several Inland Steels strewn around the country." U.S. Steel could—and should—be broken up into several smaller companies without losing anything except its monopoly power.

The studies of California economist Dr. Joe Bain show that an automobile manufacturing company need produce only 300,000 to 600,000 cars a year to exploit all the efficiencies of mass production. His findings corroborate a statement of George Romney, when he was president of American Motors in 1958, that "all this talk about the disadvantage of lack of volume . . . is grossly exaggerated. . . . If you have 180,000 to 220,000 volume a year, you can compete effectively and efficiently in the automobile industry." By contrast, GM's 1970 sales were 4.4 million cars.

The laws are already on the books, but for years the government has contented itself with an occasional action against isolated examples of price-fixing and coercive acts of one businessman against another.

It's like the practice during Prohibition in Oklahoma; a sheriff, every now and then, would make a big show of raiding a selected bootlegger and publicly destroying his wares. The papers would carry front-page pictures of the sheriff with ax in hand, standing over the broken bottles, while whiskey ran in the gutters. Then everyone would relax again. That's pretty much what government has done from time to time in regard to antitrust enforcement.

To define the basic evil of monopoly in more sharply drawn numerical terms and to make it mandatory for officials to carry out the law, I introduced new deconcentration legislation in the Senate in the fall of 1971. The bill was patterned after the 1968 recommendations of President Johnson's Task Force on Antitrust Policy.

In any industry in which there are $500 million or more in sales and where four or fewer firms account for 70 percent or more of the market, the shared-monopoly companies would have to be broken up into smaller, competitive companies, none of which would control more than 12 percent of industry sales. The legislation provides for a "scale-economies" defense if it can be shown that deconcentration would produce inefficiencies and higher consumer prices.

In 1972 the New Democratic Coalition, whose original membership had been organized around former supporters of Eugene McCarthy and the late Senator Robert F. Kennedy, fully endorsed the need for redistribution and deconcentration. With NDC help, we made a fight on shared monopolies in the preconvention sessions of the platform committee of the Democratic party.

Opponents won the battle in the drafting subcommittee. But a brilliant young legislative assistant on my Senate staff, James C. Rosapepe of Virginia, took the question to the full platform committee and reversed the drafters by a substantial majority vote. The official 1972 platform of the Democratic party called for breaking up the shared monopolies, specifically listing as examples the automobile, steel, and tire industries. It was the first such plank in a major party platform since 1912. It's too bad this was not a crucial issue in the 1972 presidential campaign.

Not many people were surprised when former Treasury Secretary John Connally announced in 1972 that he was heading up a group of "Democrats" for President Nixon's reelection. He and President Nixon saw eye-to-eye on special investment tax credits and favorable accelerated depreciation rules for big business. They both agreed that the "hobby farming" and oil and gas depletion provisions in the tax laws were not loopholes at all, but are good for "everybody."

When he headed the Treasury Department, Secretary Connally was asked by a reporter whether vigorous enforcement of the antitrust laws would play any part in the Phase II extension of wage and price controls. "Very frankly," he answered, "the matter has not been discussed at all."

The New Populism

It must be discussed. And it must be done. Otherwise, what we are pleased to call a competitive economic system will continue to mean competition for working people and socialism for the rest.

CHAPTER

IV

The Government's Better than a Cotton Crop and Twice as Easy to Pick

My father, Fred B. Harris, is a small farmer in southwestern Oklahoma. He had some strong words for me not long ago: "You and those politicians have just about helped us small farmers out of existence."

I recounted this conversation to the Senate Agriculture Committee when I was the lead-off witness against the confirmation of President Nixon's nomination of Earl L. Butz to be Secretary of Agriculture. I led the fight in the Senate against this nomination, and we came within a few votes of defeating him.

What was most important here was that, for the first time in years, the Senate was concentrating on the real issues in agriculture, not just on the adequacy of the subsidy program.

When we had that particular conversation, my father and I were in his pickup, driving around the rural area near his home. He now owns—together with the mortgage company—the small farm where he lived as a boy, after he and his family moved from Mississippi to Oklahoma as sharecroppers. He has considerable satisfaction in knowing that he now farms for himself. What he makes is his—except that he doesn't make much.

My father knows every section line, every country road, every creek, and every farm in a couple of counties. He knows the land in the area the same way he knows cattle and horses. If one steer out of two hundred in a pasture is missing, my father knows it immediately, and he can describe the missing one in meticulous detail.

"That motley-faced steer with the broken horn is gone," or "That ol' brindly heifer that lost her calf has got out"—I've heard him say something like that many times.

"Right here, on this corner, was where I went to school," my father told me as we drove along. There was nothing left to mark the place, except a few old, dying locust trees and the bare skeleton of a concrete foundation.

Then I remembered an experience I'd had while campaigning in another part of the state. I'd met a white-haired old man who told me that, years ago, he had come to that same school as a commercial photographer to take the official school picture. The old man remembered one bright little boy in the front row who wore a pocket watch and chain. The boy's name was Harris, and the old man wondered whether it had been my father. I asked him about it.

Yes, he was that bright little boy. My father remembered the picture, and he remembered the pocket watch. He said he wished he could have finished school. He went only through grade school, because that was all they offered in the area, and, since he was the oldest boy

79

in the family, he had to stay home to help with the farm work. He liked school, he said, and today he is an avid reader of any history book he can get hold of.

I didn't always think my dad was very smart—perhaps that's not an unusual attitude for growing boys. I do remember now, looking back on it, that when he was buying a farmer's cattle he could drive into a field—I saw him do it a good many times—and right away figure a price for the whole herd, maybe as many as forty or fifty head altogether. Sometimes he'd figure a little with a pencil on the back of an envelope or on a scrap of paper, but mostly he did it in his head. He judged the weight and quality of each animal, multiplied the weight by the market price for that type of animal quoted in Oklahoma City that day, then added up the individual figures to a sum to be offered for the whole herd. It's quite an achievement, when you think about it. As time has passed, I have realized that my father is pretty smart in a lot of other ways, too.

When we were driving around, he would often point out a place where a few scraggly evergreens and a cement cellar showed where a house had been. "So-and-so use to live there," he would say, or "The such-and-such family farmed that old place for Mr. So-and-so." As recently as twenty years or so ago, he told me, a family lived on virtually every quarter section of land, every 160 acres. Now you are lucky to find one family on every ten quarters.

"Too much of what the politicians have done to help the small farmer has wound up making the big, rich farmer bigger and richer," he said. "There's something wrong with your programs. They haven't helped the little farmer much; they've actually helped drive him off the land."

When I recounted this story to the Senate Agriculture

Committee, I told them I didn't want to believe it at first. But my father was right. And he still is.

He's one of the lucky ones. Somehow he's managed to hang on by working for other people—driving a bus, driving a truck, following the harvest. When I was in grade school, we baled other people's hay. We followed the cotton out to the plains of west Texas. Later, he harvested wheat from Oklahoma to North Dakota. I went with my dad on that trip nine summers in a row.

I remember that wheat was selling then for slightly more than it brings now, but farmers paid only about half what they pay today for machinery and labor.

Dr. Butz, who had been assistant secretary of Agriculture under President Eisenhower and then had gone to Purdue University, a land-grant college, to work in agricultural education, extension, and research, had a somewhat different point of view from my dad's. He was noted for his philosophy that farmers must adapt or die.

"Too many people are trying to stay in agriculture that would do better someplace else," Butz told the *Record-Stockman* in 1955. More farmers will and should leave the farms for other jobs "if the politicians will stay out of their hair," he told *U.S. News & World Report* in 1957.

Adapt or die. But those who didn't adapt, didn't die either. They moved to the city. I saw it myself in Oklahoma. Wheat farmers of western Oklahoma went to Los Angeles and Detroit. Chicano farm workers went to Denver and Phoenix. Black farmers and workers moved to Milwaukee and Newark. Cotton farmers from the hills of eastern Oklahoma left for Chicago and Cincinnati. Native Americans relocated in Cleveland and San Francisco.

And as they and their families left, a lot of small towns and communities began to dry up too. The picture show was boarded up. The implement dealer sold out to his competitor. The dry-goods store didn't reopen when its owner died. The furniture dealer moved to a larger town. The lawyer went to work for an oil company. No new doctors came to replace the old ones. And the kids graduated from high school and drove away in their graduation suits and dresses, looking for jobs.

I've seen this problem from the city angle, too. Mayor after mayor told us on the Kerner Commission the same thing over and over. In-migration had swollen their problems—housing, unemployment, transportation, education, crime—out of all proportion.

To some extent, this mass relocation of people was a conscious policy. "It is generally agreed that it is neither socially desirable nor economically feasible to try to arrest or even slow down this trend," a U.S. Department of Agriculture study declared as recently as 1966.

There are only 3 million farms today, half as many as in 1904. Half those remaining are small farms, but they account for only around 8 percent of all farm sales.

Every week for the past thirty years, 2,000 farm families in America have packed up and moved on to the city. And every time 6 farm families left—300 or so times a week—a small-town merchant locked up and moved on too.

Thirty million Americans left rural areas over the last thirty years—10 million a decade. They didn't leave because they wanted to. A recent survey shows that more than half of all Americans say they would rather live in small towns and rural areas, but only one-third actually do. Many people were forced to leave the farms and small towns because they couldn't make a living staying where they were. And today 800,000 more people a year face up to the same hard reality—and they move.

Now more than 70 percent of all Americans are stacked and packed onto less than 2 percent of the land.

Meanwhile, half of the remaining farmers, 14 million, have annual incomes below $3,000. A third of them are over fifty-five years old.

Most liberals didn't consciously approve of this policy, but what they did was often just as devastating. They acquiesced in or supported government programs and policies that intervened against competition and subsidized the wealthy and corporate farmers. The resulting bigness is not natural in agriculture. It's unnatural. Big farmers are not more efficient at farming. They are more efficient at farming the government.

The U.S. Department of Agriculture has itself said that the one-family and two-family farm is still the most efficient farm unit. Their studies show that all economies of scale possible are reached at about 1,500 acres for cotton, less than 1,000 for corn and wheat, and 110 acres for peaches.

Bigness in American agriculture is no more inevitable than a communist nation's decision to create massive state farms. And the result for the independent farmer and farm worker is the same, whether it's the state or the corporate interests that control the countryside: the farmers have little power over their own lives.

If the rich and corporate farmers are so efficient, why do they need the enormous government subsidies they now seek and get? The fact is that the federal farm subsidy program primarily subsidizes the rich and redistributes income and wealth in the wrong direction, just as my father thought. In effect, the government says: If you are already wealthy, you can get wealthier. If you are not wealthy, you're like the boll weevil in the song, "looking for a home."

The New Deal idea of farm subsidies was a good one in principle. It didn't seem fair then—and it wasn't fair —to leave the independent farmer, who had little market power, to the mercy of the market, when just about everybody else was being subsidized. Since the 1930s we have kept the program from year to year, trying to treat a symptom: the low and fluctuating income of the small farmer. Instead, we ought to eliminate unfair competition, created by the government, and do something about the basic cause: the farmer's vulnerability in the marketplace.

Actually, we've made the farmer's plight worse. In 1969 seven companies received more than $1 million each in farm subsidies. Fourteen other companies got between $500,000 and $1 million each. Fifty-four rich farmers and corporate farms were paid between $250,000 and $500,000 each. The taxpayer puts up $4 billion a year to help the small farmers, and most of it goes into the pockets of those who least deserve it.

Then, with Senator Birch Bayh of Indiana leading the way, the Congress in 1969 passed a $55,000 subsidy limit. What happened? Not much. The rich farmers and farm corporations put their land holdings in the names of various friends and relatives and continued to operate under complicated lease-back arrangements, still gobbling at the public trough with no real restriction. And the Department of Agriculture did nothing to stop them.

As I said at the time, I think there was a serious conflict-of-interest question here. In Kern County, California, relatives of the government farm subsidy chief, Kenneth Frick, received at least $208,000 in federal farm subsidy payments in 1971 alone. His second cousin, James Frick, who is a partner in Fredlo Farm, got $34,440 of the taxpayers' money in cotton payments. His first cousin, Fred Frick, also a partner in Fredlo Farm, got $51,660. His uncle, Lester Frick, who is a partner in Double L Farm, drew $4,676, and his brother, Howard Frick, a partner in Killdeer Farm, drew $114,000—both also in cotton payments.

The New Populism

In addition, Mr. Frick's father, Forrest Frick, is a partner in Killdeer Farm, an entity in which Kenneth Frick himself has a 40 percent interest, now held in trust by the Bank of America of Bakersfield, California.

When word about the Fricks leaked out, together with the information that no less than 467 other farms in Mr. Frick's home county were under internal investigation for violations of the subsidy program, the Department of Agriculture promised to look into the matter more closely. But nothing much ever came of the investigation. Senator Bayh continues to press for a $20,000 limitation on farm subsidy payments and for strict enforcement. He is right about his aims, but so far has been unsuccessful.

The movie actor John Wayne is a farmer, courtesy of the federal treasury. My wife, a member of the Comanche Indian tribe, has a particular reason for not caring much for John Wayne's Western movies. But neither of us think much of him as a free enterpriser. Ronald Reagan, Senator James Eastland of Mississippi, and former Secretary of the Treasury John Connally of Texas are also farmers on a big scale.

A good many big businesses are big farmers too. In 1971, our national food tab was $118 billion. But the independent farmer or the farm worker didn't bring that food to market and pocket those billions. It was agribusiness that got the money—that is, big corporations like Tenneco, Del Monte, Bud Antle, Ralston Purina, Green Giant, Safeway, Swift, Heinz, U.S. Sugar, and General Foods.

A lot of industrial giants are also beginning to harvest the profit in food. Consider Boeing Aircraft potatoes, Dow Chemical lettuce, Purex strawberries, and ITT ham and bread. American Brands produces both cigarettes and applesauce. Prudential Insurance, Goodyear Tire, and Standard Oil are also among the "brave new farm-ers."

If the tractor was the symbol of American agriculture thirty years ago, the corporate board room is the symbol today. A Ralph Nader study shows that twenty-nine cor-porations alone now own around 21 percent of all crop-land. In one state, Florida, more than one-fourth of all agricultural land is presently owned by corporations.

There is a kind of agribusiness fraternity, made up of people in the U.S. Department of Agriculture, the land-grant colleges, and the big and corporate farms. They all seem to know the fraternity password and handshake. They all help each other. They move with fraternal wel-come and ease from one sector to another.

Dr. Earl L. Butz, now Secretary of Agriculture, is one of the chief spokesmen for this agribusiness fraternity. At the time of his nomination, Dr. Butz was dean of continu-ing education at Purdue University, a land-grant institu-tion that sponsors taxpayer-subsidized agricultural pro-grams. He was also serving, simultaneously, on the board of directors of Ralston Purina, International Min-erals and Chemical Corporation, and Stokely-Van Camp, all agribusiness giants. He served for a time on the Board of J. I. Case, a large farm machinery company.

In addition to his dean's salary, Dr. Butz was paid $12,000 a year by Ralston Purina, $10,000 a year by International Minerals and Chemical, $4,800 a year by Stokely-Van Camp, and $3,000 a year by J. I. Case. He owned stock in all of these corporations except J. I. Case. And he regularly made paid lectures and speeches around the country, praising the farm policies that were in the interests of these corporations.

The agribusiness fraternity has a kind of swinging door. As Dr. Butz was leaving the board of directors of Ralston Purina to become Secretary of Agriculture, Clifford M. Hardin was resigning as Secretary of Agriculture to accept a high-salaried position with Ralston Purina.

The idea of the land-grant college was to assist the small farmer, but it has wound up, more often than not, subsidizing the rich. In the spring of 1972, when Dr. Butz was dean of continuing education there, Purdue sponsored a national symposium on "Vertical Coordination in the Pork Industry," attended by representatives of feed companies and food chains, economists, and U.S. Department of Agriculture officials. At least nine major executives of the Ralston Purina Company, of which Dr. Butz was then a director, were on hand. Part of the program at the symposium included the showing of a Ralston Purina film depicting the history of the hog industry —an industry fast being taken over by Ralston Purina. Twenty-four officials of the U.S. Department of Agriculture, including two deputy administrators, were present to hear the good news, some of which was spread by Dr. Butz as luncheon speaker. Academics, government officials, and corporate farm interests were gathered there in full force, but I doubt if small hog farmers were as well represented.

The land-grant college system was created in 1862 (the same year as the Department of Agriculture) to be the people's universities. Well over half a billion dollars a year of tax money goes to them. Purdue University spent $8 million on research in 1969. But the land-grant colleges have more and more become research clinics for agribusiness interests.

Tenneco is a huge conglomerate with $3.4 billion in assets. Its stockholders' report states that the corporation is setting up a food system based on "integration from seedling to supermarket." That's called "vertical integration," and it's the kind of monopoly that is supposed to be prohibited for industrial corporations. But it is more and more the rule, rather than the exception, in American agriculture. Monopolized vertical integration now controls the production of 95 percent of broiler chickens, 75 percent of processed vegetables, 70 percent of citrus fruits, 55 percent of turkeys, 40 percent of potatoes, and 33 percent of fresh vegetables—forcing more and more independent farmers off the land or reducing them to contract laborers for the corporations.

These facts are brought to light in a book, *Hard Tomatoes, Hard Times,* a crushing exposé of the failure of the land-grant college system, written by Jim Hightower of the Agribusiness Accountability Project. Hightower shows how the land-grant colleges use tax funds for underwriting agricultural technology for the farmers with the highest income, and how the colleges have ignored the independent farmers and their rural communities. Among other things, agribusiness and the colleges have helped develop a hard tomato that can be picked green by machines and chemically ripened afterward. It doesn't taste very good, but it's highly profitable for the mechanized corporate farmers. They've helped develop a big-breasted, fast-developing, chemically fed chicken. The meat tastes a little better than sawdust, but it makes a lot more money for the corporate chicken-raisers.

Agricultural research funds are being spent on the study of everything from golf courses to Astroturf—and little of the money Congress intended for the benefit of the independent farmer ever does anything for him.

The U.S. Department of Agriculture's own research figures show that less than 5 percent of the total research effort at agriculture experiment stations goes to help rural people, while the other 95 percent goes to aid automated, integrated, and corporatized agriculture.

But the land-grant college subsidy is only a small part of the special help the government gives rich farmers and farm corporations, enabling them to compete unfairly with small farmers. There is a huge tax subsidy. Doctors, lawyers, and actors can charge off farm losses against other income. A Kansas City firm, Oppenheimer Industries, promotes tax farming for the rich. In 1972, following action by Congress that supposedly closed this "hobby farm" loophole, Oppenheimer proudly announced that it had 400 Hollywood star clients, a figure that it said had doubled in the preceding four years.

In citrus growing, for example, the system works particularly well. In the beginning years, before the trees are ready to bear, expenditures are capitalized, and there is an operating loss. Rich people are solicited to invest during these losing years. Then, when the trees begin to bear and there is income from them, the initial investors sell out, and the gain in value is taxed only at the reduced capital gains rate. These tax provisions are not of any help to the ordinary farmer, whose only or principal income is from farming, because he usually doesn't have any other income to charge losses against.

Conglomerates, too, charge their losses from farming operations against gains from their other businesses. Farm corporations pay an average federal tax rate of only 4.5 percent on their farm income. The tax losses in agricultural production by vertically integrated corporations can easily be covered by their huge profits in processing or marketing. The independent farmer does not have these options.

The government also provides vertically integrated agribusinesses, giant conglomerates like Tenneco, and huge corporations like Standard Oil a special subsidy under the labor laws. Minimum-wage and labor organization laws that govern their other operations don't apply in agriculture. The corporations are thus encouraged to expand into farming, to compete with those who actually make a living from farming. The small farmer could pay a better wage than he pays now, provide better working conditions, and recognize organized workers if he didn't have to contend with the unfair advantages presently given to his huge competitors.

The concentrated economic power in agriculture of business and industrial corporations and the rising market control of vertically integrated agribusinesses produce higher prices and lower quality for the consumer. Monopoly power is just as unwholesome in agriculture as it is in industry, but agriculture is generally exempt from the antitrust laws. A bill introduced by Senator Gaylord Nelson of Wisconsin would put a stop to the situation. A 1946 study by Walter Goldschmidt of two small communities in California—one that served a corporate farm area and one that served an area of family farms—documented the harmful effects of corporate farming on democratic and social institutions.

The corporate farming community, Arvin, was a town of employees, rather than independent entrepreneurs. It had only one-half as many business establishments, one-half as much annual trade, one-third as many schools, one-half as many service and civic organizations, and one-half as many newspapers as Dinuba, the other town. In short, Dinuba was a community; Arvin was just a place where employees resided while they worked for mostly absentee owners.

The old Populists believed that it was neither good social policy nor good economic policy for corporations to be involved in agriculture. Time has proved them right. By enacting Senator Nelson's bill—Oklahoma, North Dakota, Kansas, and Minnesota have taken steps in this direction at the state level—and by ending the tax, labor law, and land-grant college subsidies for the big and corporate farmers, America can once again become a place where farmers farm the land, rather than a country where corporations farm the taxpayers.

The public trough is also a water trough. Rich and corporate farmers have gorged themselves on public water at taxpayers' expense. It is a federal policy of long standing that water is a public resource and that the use of public funds to develop and distribute irrigation water is a proper function of government, a fair use of the taxes that everybody is asked to pay.

The Federal Reclamation Act dates back to 1902, but when it was passed, the Congress decided that it wouldn't be fair to the taxpayers to use their funds just to enrich a few big farmers. So in that Act the Congress specified that a recipient of publicly financed irrigation water could not farm more than 160 acres, or 320 acres for a husband and wife. The big landholders have violated that law since its inception, and the government has stood aside, looking the other way.

"Land monopoly is not the only monopoly, but it is by far the greatest monopoly," Winston Churchill once said. "It is a perpetual monopoly and it is the mother of all other forms of monopoly."

Nowhere is this phenomenon more evident than in California. Forty-five giant corporations own more than 3.7 million acres of farmland in that state. Many of them are not even based in California, but have headquarters as far away as New York, Pennsylvania, and Texas. Yet the corporations dominate the economy and politics of whole counties—and the lives of those who live there. A single corporation, the Southern Pacific Railroad, owns 3.8 million acres in the western states.

In one California county alone, Kings County, a single landowner, the J. G. Boswell Company, owns more than 108,000 acres. Three giant companies, including Tenneco, which is based in Houston, own nearly half of all the land in Kern County.

Fred R. Harris

I call the increase in concentrated land ownership in America the "New Feudalism," and California has always been its paradise. A German immigrant, Henry Miller, around the turn of the century assembled a kingdom of 14 million acres—three times the size of Belgium. Today Miller and Lux, Inc., the direct descendant of the original Miller's operations, is still one of California's major landowners, with more than 93,000 acres.

It should never be forgotten, either, that the original development of California, and of much of the West, resulted from the exploitation of American Indians and the serfdom of Chinese, Japanese, Filipino, Asian Indian, and Mexican immigrants. Men like Leland Stanford— whose names are today linked with philanthropy and education—built huge land empires on the backs of these exploited workers. The United States Government granted 8 percent of its total land to the railroads. The idea was that this would stimulate railroad construction and homesteading. It worked out to make the big financiers rich—and many of the railroads are still, today, in violation of the terms under which they got the land.

Land reform in South Vietnam or in Latin America has long been advocated by the liberal community in America. What's wrong with a little land reform here at home? We could start by enforcing the Reclamation Act of 1902 and the original contracts with the railroads—breaking up these huge holdings and parceling them out on easy terms to people who would live and work on the land.

And this is not just an agricultural problem. Nineteen large corporations now own 35 percent of the timberland in California. The same is true elsewhere. The beautiful Appalachian hills of West Virginia, Kentucky, and Tennessee are being ripped off—literally and figuratively—by coal, steel, oil, and other huge landholding companies through strip-mining. They are ravaging the countryside, polluting and silting up the once pure streams, destroying the fish and wildlife, and pushing the trees down the hillsides or killing them with leaching acids. They exploit some of the best and poorest people in the world, putting deep miners out of work and, through criminally low tax assessments, choking off support for local schools and other institutions.

The corporations get away with it because their vast landholdings give them the economic power to make counties, and even states, into their political fiefdoms.

In the cities it is as bad or worse. Land is power. Property taxes are mostly levied on the value of improvements, rather than on the land. The people cry for housing; land and abandoned buildings stand vacant.

The old Populists maintained that a nation that believed in the right of property ought to be a nation where ordinary people had a chance to own some property. They advocated a graduated land tax and a homestead law to encourage the widespread ownership of small holdings on easy terms. The New Populism believes that it is time to take up that cause again.

But ridding the small farmer of the extra burden he carries because the government subsidizes his big competitors is not enough. The fundamental problem of independent farmers—their lack of market power—will still remain. And just trying to solve the problem by subsidizing independent farmers, to make up a little for the subsidization of big farmers, is going about it backward. Out-migration from rural areas and the growing list of failed farmers show that the independent farmer cannot depend upon a benevolent government for his fair share in the fruits of his work and investment. Market power is what he needs.

When a farmer produces a surplus, it's there for all to see—wheat piled up, butter in storage. When General

Motors produces a surplus, it can't be seen, but it's there nevertheless. When GM has produced all the cars the company can sell, it shuts down. GM has too much control. Independent farmers that are unorganized have none.

They must organize and bargain collectively for the sale of their products. That's the only way they are going to have any reliable power—power in the marketplace. The threat of substitutes and increased imports and the possible loss of export markets should be allowed to operate as natural safeguards on this organized economic power.

Today's concentrated economic power, in agriculture as in industry, makes worse the maldistribution of income and wealth in America. Traditional liberals must begin to listen to people like my father. They're not so dumb after all. And like my father, independent farmers are an independent bunch. They want to be free of unnecessary government controls. They want to be a part of a free enterprise system. But they know something's wrong. As Lavern Rison's song puts it, they're saying:

> The farmer is standing
> His back to the wall.
> The housewife is serving
> Hooves and all.
> The grocer's deserving
> A better break;
> But somebody
> Somewhere
> Is on the take.

That song questioned how a farmer's thirty cents a pound for pork got to be sixty cents a pound to the consumer. Its title is: "Nobody Knows Where the Sixty Cents Goes."

Now we know.

CHAPTER

V

If You Don't Move,
They Will Run over You

I'm no expert on transportation. But neither is the Interstate Commerce Commission or the Department of Transportation.

The ordinary traveler can go from New York to Washington by car, bus, plane, train, or boat. The trouble is that the people working to improve air travel, say, between those two cities give little thought to what's being done about easier travel by bus or car or train. There *is* no national transportation policy.

In a sense, everybody is an expert on transportation policy. We are all users of various kinds of transportation. The average American family spends nearly 14 percent of its budget for transportation—that's $90 billion a year for all of us together. From the viewpoint of users, we have a right to take a hard look at transportation and its problems.

Most of us don't like what we see. For many people there is little or no transportation at all. For the rest of us, the system often amounts to restricted choice, pollution, congestion, delays, and overcharging.

Transportation is a service—a service that I believe

citizens in an organized society have a right to expect. But transportation service in America today displays a strong economic class bias. Trying to remedy the situation, too many liberals fall back on their traditional trust in government subsidies and regulation. Indeed, most current suggestions for improvement tend toward more of the same—more subsidies or more regulation, or both.

The New Populism takes a different approach. There are certain objective tests that can be applied to the problems in transportation—and other services. I call these tests the "How Come" test, the "Why Not" test, and the "What If" test.

The *"How Come"* test asks: "How come we have to do this?" Are we treating symptoms or causes?

The *"Why Not"* test asks: "Why not try competition?" Is there an alternative involving free competition, less government?

The *"What If"* test asks: "What if competition is impossible?" If a government subsidy or a natural monopoly is inevitable, are there built-in ways to ensure that we get our money's worth?

Consider mass transit. A lot of time and money are being spent on the problem of getting people back and forth between their homes and their jobs. First of all, applying the "How Come" test, we should ask: "How come so many people's jobs and homes are so far apart?"

Watts, the largest black section of Los Angeles, erupted in violence in 1965. The McCone Commission was sent in to study the cause. They found that one glaring inequity the Watts residents suffered was the lack of transportation. Only 40 percent of the people in Watts had automobiles, and public transportation was wholly inadequate. The average worker left home at 5:30 A.M., changed buses five times, and paid 73 cents to get to his job in Santa Monica or some other distant neighborhood. Six years later, when I visited Watts again, the problem was just the same.

In a pool hall and then out on the streets, I talked to young men who were desperate for work. There were no jobs nearby. None of the young men had a car. Buses didn't go to the right places. Cabfare—to get around to plants and businesses even to ask about job openings—was hard to come by.

"My aunt's agreed to drive me out to a place where they say they need truck loaders," one of the young men told me. "But it only pays $1.65 an hour, and I don't know how I'm going to get back and forth to work every day, if I can get the job, since I don't have a car."

"What about riding the bus?" I asked.

"There's no bus that goes there," he replied.

When I was in Atlanta in 1971, a white woman in the white working-class section called "Cabbage Town" complained how hard it was to get to a doctor or a hospital. A black woman I talked with an hour later in the Summerhill section had the same complaint. There was no transportation at night—for emergencies—except cabs, and they were too expensive. And in the daytime, I was told, buses went to the wrong places. What buses there were all went downtown and unloaded there. Then you had to change buses to go on out to a job, provided there was a bus scheduled at all. Coming back at the end of the day it was the same thing—back downtown first, change buses, and on home, if there was a bus.

In Washington, D.C., a worker leaving the central city for a job in the suburbs spends two hours on the bus—if there is a bus.

Where are the jobs? More and more of them have moved to the suburbs. While St. Louis was losing 50,000 jobs in the city, its suburbs gained nearly 200,000 new ones. While the number of jobs in Philadelphia declined by 20,000, the number of jobs in the suburbs increased by a quarter million. From the 1950s on, a majority of *new* industrial, commercial, and trade jobs have been created in the suburbs. These new jobs, and the old ones that have moved to the suburbs, are generally the type of jobs that beginners and unskilled workers can break into with the least trouble. New jobs in the cities are higher-paid jobs that require a higher degree of training and skills.

Why does industry like the suburbs? They're cheaper—cheaper for industry.

When a company moves its plant to a suburb where there is no low- or moderate-cost housing, most of its employees can't live near the plant. The suburban jurisdiction registers a gain in two ways: it gets an increased tax base because of the new plant; and it doesn't have to provide additional residential services for the workers. The company then shows a better profit and loss statement because its taxes are lower—it doesn't have to pay so much of the costs of services for its employees: education, sewers, garbage disposal, law enforcement. Other taxpayers have to shoulder this burden.

The company is able to become more "efficient" because the location of its new plant is subsidized by the rest of us. And we have to pick up a part of the increased bill for transportation, too.

Where are the homes? Better housing is in the suburbs, and poor housing is in the central cities. That's not accidental. Government programs have helped make the situation. We put low-cost housing in low-income areas, the very areas where there are fewer and fewer jobs for those who reside there. Then the government sanctions local zoning that excludes multifamily dwellings in the suburbs and restricts residential acreage to high-cost large tracts.

The New Populism

Suburban Action Institute calls the result of these policies the "Lockout Effect." They published in 1971 a study of Westchester County, a relatively high-income area near New York City. During the last twenty years, as the number of new jobs in the county has increased, zoning against multifamily dwellings and smaller residential lots has become increasingly restrictive. The zoned population capacity of the county in 1962 was over three million people, according to the zoning laws then in effect, but by 1969 the figure had been reduced to something under two million—a 40 percent reduction. So jobs in the county increased at double the rate of the increase in the number of people who could actually live there. The end result was that during the last twenty years the number of those commuting *out of* the county each day for relatively higher-income jobs increased by one-half. The number of those commuting *into* the county each day for relatively lower-income jobs went up five times.

Every day now, 100,000 people get up in the morning in Westchester County and leave for work in New York City. And somewhere else 100,000 people get up each morning and leave for work in Westchester County. And they pass again in the opposite directions at the end of the day. The experts look at all these people commuting back and forth and say, "We have a helluva transportation problem here!"

The New Populism holds that government sanction of racial and class barriers in housing is a prime cause of the transportation crisis. If these barriers were knocked down and if we stopped subsidizing industry's flight to the suburbs, it wouldn't be necessary to pollute the air with so much automobile exhaust and tear up so many neighborhoods with freeways. And transportation problems would become much more manageable. While treating symptoms, we ought to act against causes, too.

Even with the shift in the location of industry, though, the great majority of jobs in the central city are still held by people who live there. And most of the workers in the central city do not have automobiles. Despite these facts, most urban freeways and transit systems have been built to serve suburban residents.

Privately owned mass transit systems go where there are people who have the money to pay. So do public transit systems. Most commuters traveling from Westchester County into New York City ride the commuter trains. But most of those coming into Westchester County for the lower-income jobs have to drive, despite the fact that these workers are least able to afford automobiles. That's because mass transit schedules and the location of terminals are generally designed to serve suburbanites, rather than city dwellers.

The new Bay Area Rapid Transit system of San Francisco is a case in point. BART is a model for other systems being planned. But there was built into even this newest transit system a class bias that is typical. Most of those who work in San Francisco live in the city—they constitute 75 percent of all the workers in the Bay Area. Also 75 percent of the households in the Bay Area without cars are located in the city of San Francisco. Yet sixty-seven of the BART system's seventy-five miles of track are located outside the city of San Francisco. Twenty-six of its thirty-seven stations are outside the city.

How come we have to spend so much on transportation? The New Populism, first of all, maintains that we would not need so much transportation if we were allowed to live where we work.

No doubt improved mass transit is essential. But the New Populism demands that there be no class discrimination in the design of these systems.

A more fundamental principle of the New Populism is that many people are unable to afford adequate transportation. Taxis or jitney buses, for example, would often serve them best—if they had the fare.

Now apply the "Why Not" test to transportation generally. Why not try competition? Is there a competitive alternative to the present system of subsidy and regulation? One does exist and airline travel is a good place to start explaining it.

Two or three years ago an executive of a major airline phoned urging me to introduce legislation prohibiting commercial airlines from giving away free drinks during flights. "You could make a lot of political hay with the anti-liquor people in Oklahoma with this one," he assured me. "Why, just the other day, a mother in California got mad as hell at us when her daughter deplaned drunk on the free drinks from one of our cross-country flights."

As we talked a little further, I discovered that we both agreed the government had no business stepping in to prohibit individual drinking. But, later in the conversation, it finally became clear to me that what the executive really wanted was for his airline to be able to *sell* rather than give away liquor. He was afraid that other airlines would not voluntarily change. So he wanted the government to order *all* airlines to do what his airline desired to do. Then his airline would not be at a competitive disadvantage.

This man's goal was relatively unimportant, but his fear of competition—and his desire for government to prevent it—is all-pervasive throughout the airline industry. Further, his attitude affects a lot more than in-flight drinks. It's the price of an airplane ticket that's most at stake.

The federal government, through the Civil Aeronautics Board, severely restricts the establishment of any new airlines. It sees its job as that of protecting the lines already in the business. It protects them from competition from other types of transportation. And it cuts down competition within the industry, between airlines. The CAB sets fares, limits the formation of new airlines, and approve mergers of existing airlines.

In California, where regulation has been at a relatively low level for airlines that operate solely within the state —and are therefore not subject to CAB control—competition produced dramatic results. On lines operating between Los Angeles and San Francisco, for example, coach fares were cut in half. And the lines show much more efficient and full use of their equipment and manpower than the interstate carriers. A real measure of the California lines' success is that there has been a substantial drop in the coach fares charged by major interstate airlines that serve the same points in California.

Despite these clear lessons, or perhaps because of them, the CAB continues to move in the other direction, away from competition.

In 1970, for example, the twelve major U.S. airlines were carrying less than 55 percent of their passenger capacity on domestic flights. Common sense should have dictated that the number of passengers would be increased by cutting fares and reducing flights on the glamour routes that are heavily overscheduled. Instead, the big airlines asked the CAB for even higher fares. The CAB agreed. It granted a 6 percent increase, and air travel was thereby further deterred.

There is clear evidence, also, that profitability does not increase with size. Continental is one of the industry's smaller airlines, but it has consistently shown a profit, while the big ones, such as Pan Am and TWA, struggle to stay ahead. Even so, the CAB has approved merger after merger, most recently the Allegheny-Mohawk combination. The result of CAB merger policy is less and less competition in the airline business.

Some say the only answer lies in getting better qualified, more impartial, and public-minded members appointed to the Civil Aeronautics Board, while we continue to pump millions of subsidy dollars into building more airports and other facilities for the big airlines to use. But in this instance history suggests that, through one means or another, those who are regulated always seem to wind up dominating the regulators.

Our best hope is in reducing regulation, in remembering our stated belief in free enterprise. There is no reason why competition can't work in the airline industry. It is not naturally monopolistic. But government action has created a system of monopoly. Ending the CAB's power to set fares or limit the number of airlines—coupled with enforcement of the antitrust law—would, at last, make fares and service subject to natural market pressures. And the need for government regulation and subsidy would lessen as well. Airline customers would have more economic power in the marketplace; they would become the natural regulators.

The same principle applies to surface transportation—buses, trucks, barges, and trains. What we have is: heavy subsidization; government protection against competition between types of transportation, and between companies in the same field; and increasingly concentrated ownership and economic power. To the consumer, this means inefficiency, inflated costs, and poor service—on top of higher taxes.

Transportation has never been a free enterprise industry. It has always been subsidized. The first bill to pass the U.S. Congress in 1789 was an act to underwrite the cost of building a canal for private companies to move freight by water. Since then billions and billions of federal funds have been spent for water transportation. I entered the Senate as the successor to the greatest all-time proponent of federal subsidies for the development of water transportation, the late U.S. Senator Robert S. Kerr. I came to Washington as a supporter of the federal program then under way to make the Arkansas River navigable in Oklahoma and Arkansas. And we got that project through. The barge lines were not made to pay a user charge to help pay for the new project from which they profited because, it was said, competitive forms of transportation didn't have to repay *their* subsidies. That's the "Highest Common Denominator" argument, all over again: new subsidies to balance out old subsidies. Later on, I learned that you can't ever get even that way. It's better to cut out the initial subsidy.

I came to the Senate, too, as a member of the "Highway Lobby." I'd grown up in Oklahoma at a time when highways were a system of chug holes and death traps. I had helped push too many cars out of the mud. I had answered more than enough telephone calls late at night and learned that another relative or friend had been killed on a narrow bridge. Later, though, I became aware that the $60 billion we've spent in federal funds on highways, a majority of it on the interstate system, benefits commercial truckers most—and that they don't pay their way.

But truckers more than pay their way in lobbying expenditures. They spend $5 million a year to prevent any change in the Highway Trust Fund. The Fund comes from highway-user taxes and is earmarked for highway spending. These highway-user taxes are levied in such a way that the truckers pay only about 80 percent of the extra cost of building highways strong enough to carry heavy trucks. The ordinary motorist is made to subsidize the trucking industry by paying a disproportionate share of what it costs to build highways stronger than those needed for passenger cars.

And, of course, the railroads got their big start with the subsidy of federal land grants. Men like Leland Stanford, Mark Hopkins, and Cornelius Vanderbilt made fortunes from resulting railroad land sales, railroad construction, and freight rates swollen by monopoly power. For a long time thereafter, living down that history, railroads shunned additional subsidies. But in recent years the lure of federal money has proved too attractive.

The Interstate Commerce Commission was created in the late 1800s to control the monopoly power of railroads. Competition was too weak or didn't exist at all. Today, though, the initials ICC could well stand for "I Curtail Competition." A good example is the yak fat case. In 1965 Thomas Hilt, a Lincoln, Nebraska, trucker with both a sense of humor and a point to make, notified the ICC that he was going to start hauling yak fat from Omaha to Chicago for $9.00 a ton. You would think that competition in hauling yak fat couldn't hurt anybody very much. But competition of any kind, or even the threat of it, worries the ICC no end. So they immediately asked the railroad's rating bureau for comment.

Again, you would think that the railroads shouldn't fear competition in hauling yak fat. Nevertheless, they made a study (one wonders how) and in due course reported to the ICC that $9.00 a ton was too cheap a rate —that it ought to be at least $12.50 a ton. The ICC solemnly notified Mr. Hilt of this attack on his competitive plans and asked for a response.

At that point, Hilt let the matter drop. For one thing, he·didn't know where to find any yak fat closer than

Tibet. And he had made his point. Under the standard philosophy of the ICC, the question had not been whether $9.00 a ton for hauling yak fat from Omaha to Chicago was a reasonable rate, but whether supposed competitors would agree to it. The ICC believes its basic duty is to preserve every form of transportation against competition from another.

It also protects truck companies against competition from other truck companies, railroads against competition from other railroads, barge lines against competition from other barge lines, and bus companies against competition from other bus companies.

The ICC permits railroads and truckers to get together on common freight rates and lets them set industry-wide price agreements. It restricts the number of barges and trucks that can operate on specific routes, and it limits the commodities that certain truckers can carry.

In short, the agency set up to regulate monopoly power in transportation has become its greatest defender. And it encourages increased concentration. Greyhound and Continental Trailways almost entirely dominate the intercity bus industry today. They have been allowed to gobble up smaller, competing companies. Now we have two giant bus lines that are only minimally competitive with each other.

The ICC has approved merger after merger in the trucking industry too. Every year there are fewer, bigger truck companies. It's hard for new companies to get a license to enter the business. And if one truck company wants to extend its service to compete with another company already serving a particular route, ICC policy is such a barrier that it's often easier for the companies to merge or for one to buy the other. There is no evidence whatsoever that bigger trucking companies are more efficient. To the contrary, the evidence is that the lack of competition in the trucking industry means poorer service and higher rates. Yet trucking company mergers are almost routinely approved.

With railroads it's the same story. From 1957 on, there has been a wave of railroad mergers, all on the grounds that greater efficiency and better service would result. The biggest was that of the New York Central and Pennsylvania railroads. The Penn Central—owning $3 billion in railroad assets and $3.5 billion in real estate and manufacturing—was the gargantuan result. What happened? The Penn Central went broke.

Studies show that a railroad with over 20,000 employees is too big for efficient management. Research and development lag, too. American industry, generally, spends over 4 percent of revenues on research and development. The transportation industry spends less than 1 percent, and the railroads don't even come up to the transportation industry average.

Who owns the railroads? We don't know—and the ICC makes no effort to find out. Holding companies and conglomerates are moving in. And the old practice of holding railroad stock in "street names" that conceal true ownership continues unabated. Some railroads own stock in other railroads. Interlocking directorates give some of the largest shippers a large share in control of the railroads they use. As the number of railroads shrinks, the evidence is that ownership has also become increasingly concentrated in the hands of fewer and fewer individuals, banks, and insurance companies.

The traditional American free enterprise argument that lack of competition results in inefficiency and poor, overpriced service has been proved beyond a doubt in the case of railroads. It's a routine matter that cars are lost, or held up in switching, or delayed en route, or sent to the wrong destinations. Passenger service has all but been eliminated. The Penn Central merger was supposed to have produced $100 million in savings, but what it produced was a giant so awkward that it couldn't even tie its shoes. Irate customers took at least $20 million of their business elsewhere. And the Penn Central went bankrupt.

Railroad tracks are falling apart. Maintenance is a mess. And there were more than 8,000 major railroad accidents in 1968 alone—double the annual rate of just seven years before.

Why not try competition? A Brookings Institution study in 1971 declared that competition in the transportation industry would reduce freight rates by 20 percent. It cited the fact that when the ICC's power to set rates for hauling poultry and frozen fruits and vegetables was curtailed in the mid-1950s, freight rates went down between 20 and 59 percent on the exempted items.

There is plenty of other such proof. American Farm Lines is an Oklahoma-based farm trucking cooperative. Several years ago it was hauling food products *from* the West Coast, and the Defense Department awarded it business carrying ammunition *to* the West Coast. At the time the Defense Department was highly dissatisfied with the shoddy service, inordinate delays, and overcharging it was getting from other carriers. When American Farm Lines got the Defense Department contract, the truck companies and railroads screamed like mad. But, fortunately for the taxpayers, they lost out. Despite the fact that American Farm Lines began to carry only a small portion of the total freight involved, its competitive service and rates caused other carriers to shape up at once. Delivery time was cut dramatically. Service became much more reliable. And freight rates paid by the government on the various items involved dropped between 7 and 40 percent.

Nonregulated privately owned carriers are just as stable and long-lived as those that are regulated and are noncompetitive. And uncontrolled rates have tended to remain low, while the rates on regulated commodities have gone up. It's clear that competition *will* work.

A healthy, competitive transportation industry would reduce the need for subsidy—and give the consumer more travel options.

Railroads, for example, historically resisted every plea for improved passenger service on the grounds that the demand was not there. The saying went, "Pigs may squeal but they don't squawk"—live freight may be noisy but it doesn't write to the papers. Thus the railroads tried to eliminate what demand there was. But the Metroliner service, instituted between Washington and New York in 1969—despite the fact that its bumpy track and moderate speed were no match for a first-rate train like the Tokaido Liners in Japan—ran 75 percent full during its first year. It carried 700,000 passengers at an average rate of one hour faster for the two-hundred-mile route than other passenger trains.

Earlier, the number of passengers on the popular Eastern Airlines shuttle between Washington and New York had been increasing at a rate of between 3 and 15 percent a year. But the air shuttle gained less than one-half of 1 percent in passengers during the first year after the Metroliner went into operation.

Elsewhere, because of limited options—without this competition—airlines were stacking up in ever-higher concentric circles above every major American airport. The taxpayers were spending billions to try to keep up with the rush. They were spending, too, to build more and more superhighways.

Senator Mike Mansfield of Montana decided to do

something about poor railroad service in his state, high rates, and an annual boxcar shortage during wheat harvest. The railroads said they needed more money to buy more boxcars and locomotives. But the problem is not the need for more boxcars; it's the need to use them more efficiently. The average freight car earns money only about 5 percent of the time, moves only thirty-two miles a day, and makes only nineteen trips a year. If existing boxcars were used only 3.5 percent more, no more of them would be needed at all.

Senator Mansfield concluded that the answer was not increased subsidy and more noncompetitive regulation. He went to the basic cause of the problem: lack of competition. Abolish the ICC altogether, he said. That and determined action against concentration, he and others rightly maintained, was the simple home remedy needed.

But the railroads had other ideas in mind. Historically, the railroads have argued for less government regulation, while the truck companies and barge lines have supported regulation. In recent years, however, railroads have become addicted to federal subsidies. So in 1971 they finally made a deal with the trucks and barges. They would all support increased subsidies. And they would all support the continuation of noncompetitive government regulation.

No one noticed at first when the Association of American Railroads set up ASTRO—America's Sound Transportation Review Organization—to launch a saturation public relations campaign for public support of the transportation industry's new legislation. State chairmen and vice-chairmen were named throughout the country, then district chairmen. A speakers' bureau hit the civic club circuit with canned speeches and fancy press kits. Spokesmen appeared on local radio and television. Public officials were enlisted. Chambers of commerce were solicited. A nationwide multimedia advertising program was undertaken.

And former U.S. Senator George Smathers and astronaut Wally Schirra were hired to head up the national drive.

Results of these massive efforts soon began to show up. ASTRO succeeded in really scaring the public. "U.S. Railroads May Collapse, Smathers Says," read a *Washington Star* headline in early 1971. ASTRO was well named. Its demands were astronomical. Among other things, they needed, Smathers said, federal loan guarantees and a revolving loan fund to purchase new equipment and $600 million more in direct federal assistance.

An article appeared in *The Washington Post,* headlined "Surface Transport Industry Presents Aid Plan To Hartke." It told how railroads, trucks, and barges wanted even more—more power in the ICC to set rates on items exempted from regulation, special new tax concessions, and greater ease in the abandonment of services.

Large tax-deductible advertisements began to appear in the nation's newspapers, signed "America's Railroads —You Need Them. They Need You." The message was: "A second car, a summer place, and education for your children—all the things you want to come your way in life. They will only come with a healthy economy, carried along by a healthy transportation industry." The advertisement did not make clear, of course, that what was considered by the railroads to be a healthy transportation industry was one that received increased federal subsidies and in which there was little competition.

In early 1972, another headline in *The Washington Post* proclaimed "Rate Raise Asked By Railroads." Not satisfied with a 1971 rate increase or with a special 2.5 percent increase granted them for 1972, they wanted an additional 2 percent rate hike.

The *Washington Star* reported that "Department of Transportation Aide Favors Big Rail Systems." It quoted the undersecretary of Transportation as saying that huge end-to-end mergers of healthy railroads to create a few transcontinental rail systems made "eminent good sense."

Higher rates and more concentration. The Senate helped out by passing a special bill giving the railroad companies $2 billion more in new loan guarantees to purchase additional boxcars.

Then the television campaign started. Over and over, viewers saw the familiar face and heard the familiar voice of astronaut Wally Schirra. With eerie "space" music playing in the background, the camera would move in from outer space, toward earth, while Schirra said, "The future of transportation—from up here it appears pretty good. Down here on earth, people worry about it."

The camera would move closer down to earth through the clouds, showing the landscape, and the astronaut would say, "Because America's railroads, trucks, and regulated water carriers can't produce the money needed to modernize for the future, their future is in doubt. Nobody asked for it, but this is everybody's problem. Because if America can't deliver the goods, we'll all pay the price, *higher* prices, for fewer goods."

The camera would move still closer, revealing Schirra standing on the railroad tracks, reassuring us. "But there is hope yet," he would say. "The Surface Transportation Act."

Then the television spot would end with a closeup of the astronaut, talking to us person-to-person. "Who needs the Surface Transportation Act?" he would ask sincerely. "We all do."

I was offended by this television advertisement. I was

offended that the railroads could so blatantly propagandize the rest of us, using our own money. The cost of the advertisements were deducted for tax purposes. I was offended, too, because the ads were deceptive. They didn't tell the whole story about the Surface Transportation Act. The bill would grant special tax treatment and would increase present subsidies. It would provide new loan guarantees totaling $5 billion. It would allow rate increases up to 6 percent a year and the right to abandon services much more freely.

Robert Fellmeth and I put together a group of farm organizations that opposed the Surface Transportation Act as being blatant special-interest legislation. We demanded that NBC, the network that had carried the Schirra advertisement, grant us free air time for counterads. It agreed to do so.

When we discussed the format for our television spot, one of my staff members suggested *The Great Train Robbery* in reverse—a train pulling into a small town and the crew jumping off to rob the town. Cooler heads prevailed, and we agreed on a simple format that paralleled Schirra's. The camera showed me at some distance, walking down a railroad track, saying, "America's railroads are in trouble, their tracks are falling apart, their equipment is old, and now they have come to Congress to ask for $5 billion of our taxes to modernize, because they say they can't raise the money themselves."

"This just isn't true," I said, close up. "In the last four years the railroads have been granted rate increases worth almost $2 billion and government loans worth millions more. But, instead of using this money to modernize, many railroads have spent it on real estate, cattle ranches, and golf courses, but not railroading. And now they are asking the American taxpayer to pay for this neglect."

And then I asked the same question Wally Schirra had asked: "Who needs the $5 billion Surface Transportation Act?" My answer was different from his. "I believe America's taxpayers don't," I said. "Neither do the railroads. Let the railroads spend the money they've got—on railroading."

The railroads were not overjoyed about our counterad. But there was nothing they could do, because we had the goods on them. Railroads are into everything from aircraft companies to pipelines. Burlington Northern, for example, controls 8.5 million acres of land in fifteen states in the United States and two provinces in Canada. They are engaged in irrigated farming and grazing, manufacturing, lumbering, mining, and oil and gas production.

Seaboard Coast Line owns the Florida Publishing Company that publishes the *Florida Times-Union,* the *Jacksonville Journal,* and the *St. Augustine Record.* Santa Fe owns a trucking subsidiary, a pipeline, and an oil and gas production company.

The Penn Central is a real estate trust of the kind that Theodore Roosevelt would have busted in a minute. Among other things, it controls a company that owns 100,000 acres of development real estate in Florida and the Royal Palm Yacht and Country Club.

But it began to look as if our efforts were too little and too late. The Senate Commerce Committee approved the Surface Transportation Act—except that it cut the new loan guarantees from $5 billion down to $3 billion and added some direct federal cash for branch lines. There was only one opposing vote in the committee, that of Senator Norris Cotton of New Hampshire. "We are backing into eventual government ownership and operation of the railroads," he declared.

He was right. But it was a strange kind of ownership —with all the problems of ownership and none of the benefits. The idea was that the taxpayers would put up the money for the private gain of those who owned the railroads. They would have no control. They couldn't even find out who was getting the money, because nobody could or would tell who owned the railroads.

That brings us to the third New Populist test, the "What If" test. What if government subsidy or natural monopoly is inevitable? Are there built-in ways to ensure that we get our money's worth? There are.

First of all, it bears repeating that most of the subsidies and most of the monopoly aspects of transportation in America could and should be eliminated by permitting competition and reliance on the market. But where monopoly is inevitable or subsidy is granted, getting our money's worth—more efficient management, good service, and fair pricing—should not depend upon a benevolent government bureaucracy. That kind of faith is not justified by history.

In 1971 the government gave $140 million in federal loans and guarantees to Amtrak, a "for profit" corporation formed to improve passenger service for private gain. After spending enormous amounts for loans, professional fees, and a public relations campaign, Amtrak failed to improve passenger service perceptibly and lost $500,000 a day in its first year. The solution? The Senate voted $270 million more in direct federal aid and $315 million more in federal loans and loan guarantees —again trusting the owners to do right by the taxpayers. An investor who would put up that kind of money would demand a real share in direct control. So should the taxpayers.

If public subsidy to a private company for private gain is unavoidable, then at the very least the public should share in ownership.

A share in ownership gives *private* investors a share in control. And that's the way, too, to assure the taxpayers a voice in a private company they're asked to invest in. The taxpayers should share in profits. They should have representation on the boards of directors. One result might be that businessmen would become a little more reluctant to ask for federal handouts for private profit.

There are cases where commuter transit—and perhaps other transportation service—may be a natural monopoly. When that's true, why should an O. Roy Chalk, former owner of the D.C. Transit System, for example, be able to continue to bilk the taxpayers while raising rates and letting the quality of service offered by his privately owned monopoly steadily deteriorate? That kind of system doesn't work. Mass transit in this country is characterized by rising fares and declining ridership—and America is increasingly inflicted with "highwayitis."

If competition is impossible and a natural monopoly is unavoidable in municipal transit or in any other essential service, then the public should own the system outright. And that should be the aim of federal policies.

That's not a new idea. William Jennings Bryan said it in 1906. "The Democratic Party, if I understand its position, denies the economic as well as the political advantage of private monopoly and promises to oppose it wherever it manifests itself," Bryan said. "It offers as an alternative competition where competition is possible, and public monopoly wherever circumstances are such as to prevent competition."

That may not be the present position of the Democratic party. But it's what the New Populism advocates. And if I'm right in believing that people are smart enough to govern themselves, it's a position that will increasingly find approval with a public that is tired of hearing, "You can't get there from here."

CHAPTER
VI

Power Corrupts, and Absolute Power Corrupts Absolutely

Some Indian tribes once used petroleum as a medicine. And when I was young, we put kerosene—"coal oil," we called it—on cuts and scratches as a curative. We thought it had healing qualities.

Today the situation is reversed. Oil is making us sick—sick with pollution, to be sure, but also sick economically. Actually, the whole energy industry is itself sick with gluttony. It has devoured too much of the competition, too much of the market.

My family worked horses and mules when I was growing up. There were two kinds of animal. We called some "easy keepers," because in the wintertime when the grass was short, they stayed out in the pasture, rustling their own feed.

The other kind we called "barn horses." It was all you could do to get them out in the field to work in the morning. And the only time they showed much spirit was

117

when you headed them back toward the barn at noon or at the end of the day. Then you almost had a runaway. In the wintertime they hung around the barn, wanting to be hand-fed.

A lot of "barn horses" were smart. Some of them learned how to open granary door latches. Sometimes they'd get into the oats and eat so much that they'd founder. When that happened, we'd have to dose them with something.

The energy industry in America is like a bunch of "barn horses." It has gorged itself to the point of foundering. And it needs a good dose of New Populism.

In the beginning, there was competition in finding, refining, and selling oil and gas. "Black gold" was a fabulous bonanza for those who found it, and a gambler could hit it big. But gamblers hate odds. Improved geology reduced the risks some. But that wasn't enough for the oilmen.

Economic and political power did a much better job. The oilmen said that a busy, growing nation needed the rapid discovery of new oil reserves to fuel its continued growth, and so there ought to be special incentives for oil exploration—that was the oil industry argument. And the Congress bought it.

The oil industry was voted a special tax benefit, now worth $2 billion a year, through the oil and gas depletion allowance. People who discover oil and investors who buy or people who inherit interest in an existing oil well don't have to pay any tax at all on 22 percent of their gross income from oil, up to a maximum of 50 percent of profits. (Until 1969 the figure was 27½ percent.) One of the original arguments for the tax subsidy was that a part of gross income from oil production is actually a return of capital investment and is not really income. But that's just theory, because the exemption of this income from tax is not limited to the amount of the actual capital investment. And it is not tied to the degree to which these special profits go back into new exploration, although the other argument for this loophole was that it would encourage the finding of new oil reserves. It's just a generous subsidy.

Oil companies are allowed a second lucrative tax advantage by being permitted to write off right away as expenses their intangible drilling costs, rather than have them treated as capital investment. This procedure, again, greatly reduces the part of their income that is subject to tax.

The discovery and production of crude oil, then, has become a special kind of tax-sheltered business in the United States. And the tax encourages high crude oil prices. So if an oil company is engaged in, say, both marketing and production, it is encouraged by the tax laws to charge as much of its costs and expenses as possible to its marketing arm and run up as high a rate of profit as it can in its production division.

But how can crude oil prices be kept high if there are special incentives for everybody to get into the business? That is a question the oil companies first began to ask themselves in the 1930s. And they came up with a good noncompetitive answer: proration—that is, limiting the production of oil by state law. One aspect of proration has a logical base in that a large underground pool of oil, when discovered, may actually belong to a number of owners. And, unless restricted in some way, one owner can rapidly pump out the whole pool. Besides being greedy, this practice can also be very wasteful. In the rush by one owner to get the oil out rapidly, to the exclusion of the others, the recovery potential of the pool—the possibility of extracting the maximum amount of oil discovered—can be seriously diminished.

The states set up proration procedures to protect the rights of the various owners of any discovered oil pool and to ensure that the best conservation techniques were used in production. But the procedures failed to stifle competition sufficiently to suit the oil industry. So the proration laws went a step further. The states set up procedures to determine how much crude oil could actually be sold at an established, high market price. Then they put a lid on any production above that, halting extra production that would tend to bring the price down.

But what if one state was less restrictive than another? What if competition in one place undermined the lack of competition elsewhere? The oil companies had thought about that possible loophole, and they got the Congress to plug it up. Federal laws were passed to permit the states to agree among themselves on binding limits on crude oil production. And the Congress made it illegal to sell "hot oil"—that is, oil produced anywhere in excess of the proration limits—in interstate commerce.

The average citizen began to pay special tribute to the oil industry out of both pockets. Out of one pocket—his taxpayer pocket—he paid for the oil and gas depletion allowance and the intangible drilling cost write-off. In 1971 the eighteen largest oil companies paid only 6.7 percent of their net income in federal taxes—and the taxpayers had to make up the difference. Out of his other pocket—the consumer pocket—the citizen paid higher prices for the lack of price competition in crude oil production.

The gambler's odds were down much lower. But the fix was still not favorable enough to the oil companies. Some companies were explorers and producers. Some were refiners. Some were marketers. Such a competitive system still permitted too much risk. After all, if he were left alone, a refiner might buy from any one of several producers. A marketer might buy from several refiners. So the oil companies began to integrate vertically in order to control the flow of oil all the way from the wellhead to the gas pump.

John D. Rockefeller of Standard Oil had long since set the pattern for monopoly in the oil industry by driving some of his competition out of business and by buying out the rest. His career, repeated over and over, is a succinct history of the oil industry. And today the rate of concentration is faster than ever. Companies that produce their own crude oil enjoy increased control of the market and special tax advantages. So the Union Oil Company bought the Pure Oil Company and became the twelfth largest oil company in the country. And the federal government's Antitrust Division, despite accurate warnings that this particular merger would start a new wave of similar concentration, offered no objection.

Then Getty merged with Tidewater. Sun Oil, the thirteenth largest, and Sunray DX, the seventeenth largest oil company, combined. The fourteenth largest, Atlantic, bought the twenty-third largest, Richfield. In all, eight of America's largest oil companies disappeared after 1960. They merged with even bigger companies or were bought outright.

The abuses of the original Standard Oil Trust had produced the antitrust movement in the last century. The first landmark legislation was the Sherman Antitrust Act of 1890. But the government's memory is short. And it has stood aside while oil companies have integrated "backwards" to the oil fields themselves—buying out other producers and refiners, building and buying pipelines to the oil fields. Nearly four cents out of every dollar the average consumer spends goes for oil and gas. But when he drives up to the pump, his money gives him no market power at all.

It's a seller's market, and the sellers control it. Did you ever wonder why a filling station sells only one brand of gasoline? The system doesn't always have to work that way, and it didn't always. Originally an independent businessman could open up a service station, buy from any one of several refiners or wholesalers, and sell the product under his own name or whatever name or brand he wished. He could compete for customers by offering a better price and better service. But he can't anymore.

There was a time when the big companies owned their own outlets. Some states, beginning with Iowa, passed laws to restrict this kind of chain operation. The companies turned the restriction to their advantage. Although they still retained ownership of some of their best stations, they began to set up "independent" dealers on a franchised basis, either through sales commission contracts or, most often, through short-term leases of filling station facilities. Now a dealer will operate a single station for a huge oil company landlord, selling its one brand alone.

In this way the company gets a sure and exclusive outlet for its product. It also gets extra lobbying power, indirectly, because politicians tend to pay more attention to the entreaties of "independent" businessmen, and they tend to see gas station franchises as independent. And because it is extremely difficult for the filling station employees—who are few in number in relation to the number of separate dealers they work for—to get together and organize, the oil companies are effectively protected from unionization at the marketing level.

Suppose you want to open a new filling station and sell gasoline for two or four cents cheaper than the big company outlets. The gasoline's the same. You get it from the same refinery where the national brand-name companies get theirs. You put a big sign out in front of your station calling attention to your lower price. And business begins to boom.

But not for long. A lot of people tried doing this following World War II, at the end of gasoline rationing. But the majors wouldn't allow the practice then, and they won't allow it now.

First of all, if you try to beat them, they'll cut off your supply of gasoline. If they own the refinery, they'll refuse to sell to you until you bring your prices into line. If you are getting your wholesale gasoline from a refinery that doesn't control its own crude oil supply but has to buy crude oil from a major company, they'll make the refinery quit selling to you. They can do this by threatening to cut off the supply of crude oil the refinery has to have in order to operate.

That's one way to stifle competition. Another way is for the company to buy you out or convert you to dealer status with them, selling their brand exclusively at their established price. And when you're a dealer who's gone through a price war with the majors, you are a lot more willing to sell out, or convert—or raise your price back up again.

The majors have what they call a one-cent differential. That is, they won't let an unbranded gasoline be sold at a price more than one cent cheaper than their own brands. They will give reduced price-war prices on wholesale gasoline to their own exclusive dealers or reduce their dealers' lease payments. And, subsidizing their dealers' losses that way, they will cut retail gasoline prices, as low as necessary for as long as necessary, to bring an independent to his knees.

The majors don't compete with *each other* on retail prices. Any time you see big signs out in front of their stations, calling attention to the price of gasoline, you can be sure that you're not getting a better price for long.

The real story is that some gutsy independent entrepreneur is on his way to a bad beating.

Price wars not only reduce competition in marketing. They also encourage integration in production and refining. An independent refiner whose independent customer stations get into a price war will soon go under himself, or sell out. And even big oil companies that are only in marketing get the message, too: they must move to control their own crude oil production and refining if they are going to be able to equal the market power of their integrated competitors.

The idea of American mass marketing is that it should deliver a better-quality product to the consumer at a lower price. But the system certainly doesn't work that way in the gasoline industry. The product is virtually the same from one major brand station to another. And yet the majors resist any efforts to force them to tell the components of their gasoline—the octane content, for example. Additives are often valueless, except as advertising gimmicks.

An official of Phillips Petroleum, Stanley Learned, admitted in a Federal Trade Commission hearing that the majors exchange gasoline with each other, and he said that each company in effect puts in a pinch of something to make its gasoline distinctive. "We have an additive that allows us to advertise," he said. "I don't know whether it does anything for gasoline."

But what if a major oil company's *exclusive* dealer decides on his own to increase his sales volume by reducing the price of gasoline? He'll have that enterprising thought knocked out of his head pretty rapidly. His short-term lease is likely to be canceled, and his rent may well be raised. Or company-owned stations can reduce their prices to undersell him. The maverick dealer gets the message pretty quick—or he goes under. The message is that the so-called independent dealer for a major company is an indentured servant.

But if the dealer keeps his place, the company that holds him in bondage will give him a measure of protection. He will be protected against price wars. And he'll get the benefit of a massive national promotion of the gasoline brand he agrees to sell exclusively.

The oil and gas industry is a shared monopoly. Standard Oil of New Jersey, Mobil, Texaco, and Gulf accounted for 55.4 percent of all petroleum sales in 1970. Jersey Standard alone controlled nearly 20 percent of sales. In particular areas or regions, the company names are somewhat different, but a few of the major companies nevertheless control the market. You might see all four corners of an intersection occupied by major-brand filling stations. Why must we have so many? We don't have to have them, but the majors like it that way.

They want their own exclusive marketing outlets, because they can control them. The result is far too big a number of filling stations, with more being added all the time. And the consumer pays in higher gasoline prices for this excessive investment and expense—not to mention aesthetic and ecological costs.

A lack of competition in the gasoline industry, as in other industries, results in excessive expenditures, too, for advertising and the promotion of products that are essentially the same and are sold at essentially the same prices. Each major company tries to tie you to its own credit card, which is generally not interchangeable with those of its competitors. This obviously is a wasteful and inefficient practice that runs up costs and increases the consumer's price. Half the cards issued are either used very little or not at all, causing enormous and unnecessary extra bookkeeping and financial records.

In the past the majors have sometimes forced their

dealers to use trading stamp promotions. The dealers bore most of the cost of trading stamps, and they bear most of the cost of games and contests and special prizes and giveaway items. Consumers pay the rest of the cost. The company's profits go up through increased sales.

The law says that *forcing* a dealer to participate in such a promotional campaign is illegal. But Joseph E. Berger, a dealer for a major oil company, found out that the law is not enforced. He tired of losing money participating in the company's national promotion campaigns. So he threatened to quit sponsoring the promotions. He found out, right quick, what other dealers have found out: the company means business about promotion campaigns. Suddenly his lease was cut to six months, and he was forced out of business anyway, law or no law.

The dealer for a major company also has to carry for sale the company's tires, batteries, and accessories—known in the business as "TBA." Bob Michaud, a Texaco dealer in Maine, decided he didn't want to carry Texaco's exclusive TBA line. He came to that decision for a very good reason: he could get the same products at a cheaper price through local wholesalers. And he was aware that the Supreme Court had ruled that no dealer could be forced to carry only his major company's preferred product. But Texaco trumped up another reason and canceled his lease nevertheless.

One result of this noncompetitive marketing system is that the 211,000 filling station operators for major oil companies have an extremely precarious economic existence. The turnover rate of dealers in the gasoline industry is far higher than in other comparable industries—as many as 40 percent of the dealers in some markets change jobs every year. Shell's turnover is 26 percent, and the industry average is 24 percent.

While dealers are being pressed to the wall, consumers are paying gasoline prices that are at least 6 percent higher than they would be if marketing were competitive. And the big oil companies get bloated on the profits of protected integration, of cutting out competition all the way from the oil field to the filling station.

In late 1970 some large domestic oil producers arbitrarily raised the price of crude oil by twenty-five cents a barrel. But, you may ask, what's to keep foreign-produced oil from flooding into the United States and bringing down domestic prices? The oil companies thought of that question long before you did. For one thing, back in 1959, they got the President of the United States to institute oil import quotas by executive order. Backed up by no law, President Eisenhower simply *decreed* a mechanism for limiting oil imports to protect the domestic price. The system was justified on the basis of national security. It was said that by restricting oil imports we would encourage the finding of more oil here at home; in wartime we would not be dependent on foreign oil. Actually, the decree didn't do much for national security, but it certainly made the big oil companies more financially secure at the expense of domestic consumers.

President Nixon's Cabinet Task Force on Oil Import Control reported in 1970 that, but for these import restrictions, the U.S. domestic wellhead price for crude oil —$3.00 per barrel—would decline, over time, to around $2.00 per barrel. The task force found that American consumers were paying $5 billion more each year for oil products than they would have to pay if imports weren't restricted. Despite his pronouncements against inflation, President Nixon rejected the recommendations of his own task force for abandoning the oil import quota system.

Any President, by the stroke of a pen, could end the system. But the major oil companies are even prepared for that eventuality. Their trump card is a world oil cartel —they've been allowed to corner production, world-wide.

The arrangement goes back a long way. Jersey Standard, Royal Dutch–Shell, and Anglo-Persian (which became British Petroleum) entered into a kind of treaty back in 1928, dividing up the world market and agreeing against surplus production that might bring down the world price of oil. Since then the oil companies have become more devious in such violations of the antitrust laws, and the U.S. government has become, if anything, more lax in enforcement. Seven major companies—Jersey Standard (now Exxon), Royal Dutch–Shell, British Petroleum, Mobil, Standard of California, Gulf, and Texaco—presently control almost all of the production and marketing of Middle Eastern oil, for example.

In 1971 oil cartel companies in the Persian Gulf countries agreed to an increased cost of four cents a barrel. But they were able to jump their selling price by twenty-eight cents a barrel in the Japanese market, because they control that market. By agreement, they sell *residual* fuel oil cheaper in Europe than they sell residual fuel oil in the United States, keeping United States prices unnaturally high. In short, huge oil companies are allowed to make their own international prices and their own foreign policy.

Again, average Americans pay out of both pockets. They pay out of their consumer pocket in higher fuel prices. They pay out of their taxpayer pocket too, because, strangely enough, oil companies can deduct the U.S. depletion allowance from their *foreign* oil income. Don't forget, this provision was originally justified on the ground that it would spur the discovery of additional domestic oil reserves.

The oil companies are also allowed to reduce their

U.S. income taxes by the amount of the tax payment they make to foreign governments. This payment was considered at first a royalty, that is, a deductible business expense, not a *credit* against U.S. income taxes. But the oil companies found it enormously more advantageous financially to treat these foreign royalty payments, under agreements negotiated with the potentates of oil-producing countries, as taxes. They then got credit, not a less lucrative deduction from income, but credit against actual taxes that they would otherwise have to pay in the United States.

So, while we say that national security and national economic health depend upon finding and producing *domestic* oil, our policies actually give greater encouragement to foreign discovery and production. American oil companies, between 1959 and 1969, spent six times as much for foreign exploration as they did for domestic exploration.

International oil companies based in the United States avoid taxes on about one-half of their profits through the depletion allowance and by writing off intangible drilling costs. They avoid taxes on three-fourths of the remainder of their income through the foreign tax credit. Five international oil companies headquartered in the United States earned nearly $30 billion between 1962 and 1968. But their total U.S. income tax payment for that entire period was only $1.4 billion—a rate of just 4.7 percent.

The oil industry's plan is simple, and it has followed it to the letter. It secures federal subsidies: by the oil and gas depletion allowance; by the write-off of intangible drilling costs; and by the foreign tax credit.

It eliminates competition: by state proration, limiting domestic production; by exclusive dealership marketing; by merging with or buying competitors; by vertically integrating; and by international cartels and import quotas.

What's left? Competition from other fuels, you say. Again, the oil companies are ahead of you. There is an increasing demand for natural gas, but most domestic gas reserves are now owned by the major oil companies, including the same ones who control international oil. And the Federal Power Commission, which is supposed to regulate gas prices, is largely dependent upon the oil industry for information about reserves and the proper level of prices. In the spring of 1972 the FPC took the oil industry's word—"crisis" is the word—about a shortage in natural gas reserves and, in effect, took the lid off all gas prices. Oil doesn't have to compete with gas. Both are overpriced. And both fuel sources are owned by the same companies.

In some industries, *coal* should be directly competitive with oil and gas. And in the near future that competition ought to increase—to the benefit of the consumer—because of new processes for converting coal into synthetic gasoline through "liquification" and into synthetic gas through "gasification." But the oil companies have moved in. Gulf Oil bought Pittsburgh and Midway Coal Company. Continental, the ninth-largest oil company, purchased Consolidation, the very largest coal company. In the last ten years, seven of the largest independent coal companies have been purchased by non-coal companies. Four of these purchases were made by large oil companies that are also vertically integrated in the oil and gas business.

In addition, Exxon, Kerr-McGee, Atlantic Richfield, Shell, and Sun Oil own huge coal reserves. It's supposed to be against the law to buy up the competition, but these violations continue unabated.

And it isn't just the oil companies that are doing it. Copper companies, steel companies, and railroads, great users of coal and other fuels, are buying up coal companies and coal reserves—controlling their own supply, reducing competition.

Demand for coal has gone up at the rate of 5 percent a year during the last two years. Production has gone up at the same rate. But coal prices have increased an average of 70 percent. And they've more than doubled in some places.

In uranium it's pretty much the same. Oil companies own nearly half of all known uranium reserves in the United States. New Jersey Standard and Gulf are heavily involved in uranium and atomic energy. Kerr-McGee, by itself, owns nearly one-fourth of the total uranium milling capacity in the country.

The big oil companies are moving in on *new* energy sources also. They are buying up the oil shale and tar sands in the Rocky Mountains and Canada. Underground steam looks promising as a new power source. So a few big companies, such as Union Oil, Signal, and Getty, are rapidly gaining control of steam too, though much of it is under *public* lands in California and the other states in the West.

The main "crisis" in energy is that energy sources are monopolized. The twenty-five largest oil companies are all involved also in natural gas. Eighteen of them invest in oil shale and uranium. Eleven are in coal. Seven are in tar sands. Six of the ten largest oil companies are involved in all four major domestic fuels—oil, gas, coal, and uranium.

The twenty largest oil companies each have more than $1 billion in assets. And seven of the twenty biggest industrial corporations in America are oil companies. You can make a chart showing competition and profits in the oil industry. The competition line falls downward, *off* the chart. The profits line zooms upward—showing an increase of 13 percent in the first half of 1971 alone. Concentrated economic power means a redistribution of income and wealth in the wrong direction. It also translates into political power. The oil companies are trying to monopolize and dominate government studies of how to solve the "energy crisis."

The "barn horses" have foundered, and we've got to make them well. We've got to get them out in the pasture, rustling for their own keep. That means ending the subsidies—all of them. It means ending the government-imposed restrictions on competition. It means breaking up monopoly power; stopping vertical integration and exclusive dealerships; ending the international oil cartel; breaking up the big oil companies and their monopoly control of energy sources. It means less regulation; allowing competition between fuels; requiring pipelines to compete with pipelines, carrying oil and gas, as the law requires, without discrimination among customers.

That's a hard message to get across. The big oil companies spend millions of dollars in tax-deductible advertising to tell us what a great job they're doing toward cleaning up the environment, while they're really continuing their usual practices. They spend millions more for tax-deductible advertising to convince us that we are well served by the present system of huge subsidies and no competition. Mobil, for example, runs newspaper advertisements headed "A Stagnant Economy Is the Worst Kind of Pollution." Their message is that if the energy industry has to join the free enterprise system, economic growth will be killed.

But I come from Oklahoma, one of the biggest oil states, and my eyes have been opened to the real "energy crisis"—the lack of competition. If I can see what's going on, anyone can. The mystique of oil permeated the atmosphere when I was growing up. For one thing, it kept

The New Populism

us from taking due notice of the attendant air and water pollution.

We knew families who "hit oil" on their land. Overnight they quit raising chickens and cotton or selling cream and butter and started buying new pickups, going to beauty parlors, and getting on bank boards. We didn't envy them their sudden good luck, because it could happen to anybody—even us, we hoped.

There were jobs, too. And there was some romance to being a "roughneck" or a "roustabout." "I'm working 'evening tower' over in the new Healdton field," a fellow wearing a shiny new hard hat would say, getting admiration from the hang-arounds down at the pool hall. And the guys who drove the pickups, the "drillers," and the "toolpushers" were special kinds of idol. They chewed tobacco and talked about how many "trips" they had made on the "morning tower," and what kind of shale or sand the drilling bit was in, and how dumb the young college-educated geologist was.

Seismograph crews would come through a county, checking on underground formations. And a buzz of anticipated oil activity would spread faster and farther through the community than the miniature artificial earthquake the crew set off in the structures below. A neighbor boy with a "spudder rig" could rapidly become a big operator. Two young bootleggers in my home county pooled their earnings for a start in oil drilling and wound up owning banks.

Newspapers ran whole sections for oil news and hired reporters who did nothing but keep up with it. Everyone agreed that anything good for the oil industry was good for Oklahoma. It took me a long time—much too long— to question that philosophy. Finally I realized that what was happening was neither good for the oil industry nor good for Oklahoma. Hopefully, today, that realization is spreading.

Restoration of competition in the energy industry and ending its special subsidy favors will also have important *secondary* effects. Among other things, the price we all pay for electricity would come down remarkably. But there is much more wrong with the electric power industry in America than just the inflated price it has to pay for fuels.

The electric power industry is gargantuan. The electric companies' capital assets—now $110 billion—have doubled every ten years, a rate of growth twice as fast as the rest of the economy. They use, for example, half of all the bituminous coal produced in America.

The electric power industry is involved in three functions—generation, transmission, and distribution. Individual customers buy from a distribution system that may be privately owned, municipally owned, or owned by a cooperative. Nearly 80 percent of electric power customers buy from privately owned companies. Their combined electric bill is around $17 billion a year.

It is not a free enterprise system. The companies enjoy a "coerced" monopoly—that is, one imposed by law. You can buy electricity only from one company. By law, that company has no competition—the idea being that parallel lines and duplicative plants and services would be inefficient and wasteful. So one company is given the franchise for a guaranteed, noncompetitive territory.

Like governments, rather than private concerns, electric companies have the right of eminent domain, the right to take private property with reasonable compensation. They also sell an indispensable commodity. And they have a *guaranteed* profit. Whatever their expenses or their capital investment—whether they're held down or allowed to run high—privately owned electric companies receive a guaranteed rate of profit on their investment.

Who owns the private electric companies? It is hard to find out. We know who owns the municipal systems.

These publicly owned electric retailers serve 13.5 percent of the consumers. They're owned by the citizens in the city or power district that is served by the system. And each consumer is a voter.

We know who owns the one thousand rural electric cooperatives that serve 7.5 percent of electric customers. Each customer of a cooperative is also an owner, and each customer has one vote in the cooperative's policies.

But the situation is far different for the privately owned companies that serve nearly *80* percent of all customers. They're increasingly concentrated. Since World War II the number of private companies has been cut in half. And merger applications are increasing swiftly. We *do* know that a fourth of the two hundred largest privately owned electric companies are controlled by one or another of fifteen huge utility holding companies. But, both in the holding companies and in the electric companies themselves, owners use "street names" or "nominees" to conceal true ownership.

Stockholders' meetings are a farce. Local utility companies make a great show of putting local bankers on their boards. This little drama doesn't do anything for the interests of local customers. And it doesn't do anything for local ownership, either. The local board members are window dressing to appeal to civic pride and to give a deceptive appearance of some local control. In truth, more than 90 percent of the votes cast at any private electric company stockholders' meeting are cast by proxies.

The real owners of the electric companies are a few rich individuals and a few huge banks and insurance companies—such as Manufacturers Hanover Trust, U.S. Trust of New York, First National City Bank, Prudential Insurance Company, State Street Bank and Trust of Boston, Continental Illinois National Bank and Trust of

Chicago, Bankers Trust of New York, Girard Trust of Philadelphia, National Shawmut of Boston, the Swiss Bank Corporation, and Chemical Bank of New York.

Electric companies almost always choose *local* directors from among local bankers and local bank lawyers because of the local bank's customer relations with the big banks that control the utility companies. The local bank usually gets local utility deposits in return for voting in line with big bank—rather than local—interests.

It isn't surprising that big banks, such as the First National Bank of Chicago, run full-page ads blaming power shortages on environmentalists. Or that Chase Manhattan has issued a brochure calling for solving the "power crisis" by taking the lid off electric rates. Big banks stand to gain anytime they can increase the already swollen, protected profits of the utilities.

The traditional liberal approach has been to acquiesce in this government-imposed and privately owned monopoly system—and try to regulate it. Nationally, the Securities and Exchange Commission has exercised some lax jurisdiction over electric power holding companies and over electric utility mergers. The Federal Power Commission has been given some jurisdiction in regard to mergers and wholesale power in interstate commerce —though, in practice, the FPC has been very weak in both categories.

But most regulation of electric distribution companies is under *state* regulatory bodies. The system just doesn't work. These state commissions are notoriously understaffed. The annual budget for all of them together is no more than around $50 million—and their regulatory responsibilities cover everything from railroads to pipelines. Utility companies have the best lawyers and the best experts and an almost unlimited staff.

They also have the most political power. Their massive

power in the state capital overwhelms the regulatory bodies and makes them, uniformly, captives of those they are supposed to regulate. Many privately owned electric distribution companies operate in more than one state. Many are involved in the generation and transmission of electricity as well as its distribution. These integrated and multistate companies, especially, have an advantage over a single state agency in information, advocacy, and political power.

And the established rules for determining rates are grossly weighted in favor of the private company and against the consumer. The private company is granted a rate that will deliver a guaranteed profit. This procedure has three elements. The "rate base" is the amount of a company's total capital investment. The company is guaranteed a certain "rate of return" on this investment, after deducting "operating expenses" from revenues.

A company with a $500 million rate base would be entitled to an annual profit of $30 million, under a 6 percent rate of return. If the company had $75 million operating expenses annually, the state commission would set the charge paid by consumers at the level that would guarantee the company annual revenues totaling $105 million, plus whatever is necessary to cover their income and revenue taxes. So, after the deduction of its $75 million operating expenses, the company would have a fairly safe yearly profit estimate of $30 million.

The same company, with a $500 million rate base and a profit of $30 million, can raise its profit to $36 million simply by increasing its capital investment, the rate base, to $600 million.

Electric companies can almost manipulate these figures at will. Four states have no regulatory commissions at all. Some states that have regulatory commissions approve whatever customer charges and expenses the electric company suggests. More than a dozen state regulatory agencies allow utility companies to assign what's called a "fair value" to company property, instead of actual cost. In some states electric companies increase their rate base by buying land or businesses. And they have no great incentive to hold down the cost of what they buy or build. If the rate base—the capital investment of the company—goes up, revenues and profits will also go up.

If the rate of return goes up, revenues and profits also go up. The theoretical rate of return allowed on investment by most state commissions is 6 percent—a rate that is said to be sufficiently attractive to buyers of the bonds or stock of the company. But if the company with $500 million in rate base has an *actual* rate of return of 8 percent, say, its guaranteed profits will go up from $30 million to $40 million. And most of the big companies have actual rates of returns in excess of 7 percent. In recent years, fifty-five companies were shown to have rates of return of 8 percent or more. Twenty enjoyed 9 percent or more. The actual rates of return of three were 10 percent or more.

Here's the way it happens: the state commissions—under the "water over the dam" rule—regularly ignore the fact that revenues often prove to be greater, and operating expenses somewhat less, than the company's original estimates in the initial rate case. When an isolated state commission does act against these later overcharges, the resulting rate reductions are not made retroactive. The guilty company pockets the excessive profits it has already earned, but it would argue in justification that rate increases are not retroactive either.

Operating expenses are passed along to electric customers. So in a rate case an electric company never underestimates what operating costs will be. It overestimates, systematically. Then, afterward, the company doesn't reduce the customer charges if, for example, the interest it pays or the taxes it remits go down—unless a rare state regulatory agency forces it to do so.

The companies wind up with a lot of extra cash this way. They contribute some of it to charities and philanthropies. They gain dominant local and political support because of these donations, although the customers usually pay the bill.

Though there's no competition in the electricity market, the companies spend a lot of their money for advertising and promotion—and they usually pass this cost right along to the customer in increased rates. If you're in the grocery business and spend more on advertising than you earn in revenues, you'll go broke. Not so in the electric companies. Charging the money to consumers as operating expenses, the electric companies advertise like crazy on public issues and against environmental action. They equate themselves with everything that is American and patriotic—from the Statue of Liberty to the Flag. They use their customers' own money, through increased electric bills, to convince the customers—as voters in the political process—that privately owned electric companies are "free enterprise" and that municipally owned systems and rural electric cooperatives are wasteful and socialistic.

Not only that, but they push hard to increase the consumption of electric power, while they also, strangely enough, spread the alarm of an impending "power crisis." They do this because more power use and more customers require more capital investment, an increased rate base—and increased profits.

They arrange tie-ins with builders of "all-electric" homes, and they give special, lower rates to heavier users —all encouraging the increased consumption of electricity. Then they invest more capital in power plants and lines for an increased rate base and increased profits.

At the same time, they go right on producing 50 percent of the total of the deadly sulfur dioxide in city air and nearly 30 percent of all our air pollution. Coal-burning power plants may be spewing out as much as 150 tons a year of mercury. Yet electric power companies only spend one-fourth of 1 percent of their operating revenues on research and development. They spend eight times that much on advertising alone.

The result is excessive profits—twice the rate for firms in competitive industries. And the electric companies overcharge. Most people who are concerned might say: hold down rate increases. Actually, rates should be dramatically *reduced.*

What's to be done? First, let's try the "Why Not" test. Is there a way to ensure greater competition? There is, particularly in generation and transmission. One hundred companies now generate almost all of the electricity in the country. When the Justice Department filed an antitrust suit against Tampa Electric Company and Florida Power Company to break up their agreement not to compete in the agreed-upon wholesale power market of the other, the municipally owned Bartow system was immediately able to buy power at a lower rate. Companies that generate electricity ought to be required to compete with each other. That's the law.

And we ought to expand the number of publicly owned generation systems, now limited to two—the Tennessee Valley Authority and the Bonneville Dam on the Columbia River. These and cooperative-owned systems should be encouraged, so there'd be more of a competitive yardstick to apply to wholesale power prices.

Generation systems should not be able to integrate vertically to control *distribution* markets. That practice presently allows the kind of market dominance and stifling of competition the law is intended to prevent. Electric distribution systems should be freely able to buy competitively from a number of electric power sources.

Electric *transmission* companies, common carriers, should be made to obey the law that now is supposed to require them to carry— "wheeling," it's called—the electric power of other generation and transmission systems. In 1969 the Otter Tail Power Company, a private transmission company, refused to sell and transmit power to several municipally owned utilities in Minnesota and North and South Dakota. The Federal Power Commission said it couldn't do anything about the decision.

Senator Lee Metcalf of Montana has taken the Otter Tail Company to court. He rightly advocates that generation and transmission systems be required to interchange, pool, and transmit electric power, under a national "power grid," freely and without discrimination among customers. Privately owned generation and transmission companies have the use of every possible dodge to hold up power for municipal systems and electric cooperatives. They do the same with smaller *private* distribution companies, forcing them to sell out or build their own duplicating and expensive generation and transmission facilities.

But most electric *distribution* systems *are* natural monopolies. And we're back to the "What If" test. What if competition will not work? Why should a few huge banks and insurance companies and rich investors—with captive consumers and captive profits—be guaranteed by law to get richer, while the literally powerless mass of consumers pay more and more and have no control? The companies shouldn't have those advantages.

We ought to remove the government barriers preventing increased ownership of electric distribution systems

141

by cities, public power districts, and cooperatives. Laws that bar rural cooperatives from owning city electric systems should be stricken down. State laws that make it difficult for cities to own their own electric systems should be repealed. In Oklahoma, for example, the power lobby was able to write into the *constitution*, at statehood, a prohibition against a city issuing revenue bonds—as opposed to general obligation bonds—to purchase or build, and own, a power distribution system. Private companies can borrow on their expected revenues and utility assets, without pledging the taxing power. Why shouldn't cities be able to do so too?

If private generation and transmission systems truly had to compete with each other, as the law is supposed to require, and with an increased number of publicly owned systems, excessive prices and excessive profits would come down immediately, and service would improve. The private companies would have to respond to the market. Consumers would benefit even more if cities and cooperatives could own more of the natural monopoly *distribution* systems, without having their electric power or their credit cut off.

Customers of public and cooperative electric systems pay about one-third less for every kilowatt of power they buy than do customers of private companies. People would no longer stand for gross overcharges by private utility companies, if they had a choice—and if they had more ready examples, nearby and at hand, of the better service and the lower rates of comparable municipal and cooperative electric systems.

Natural pressures would come into play. The excessive rates and excessive profits, high operating expenses, and wasteful practices of the privately owned systems would come down. Or else the people would take over their own electric systems.

CHAPTER VII

The Money Changers Own the Temple

Growing up in small-town Oklahoma, I have two early memories about money.

Several times when I was a boy, I went with my father to the local bank. This was more than a place to deposit and borrow money; it was almost a kind of religious institution. Its brick and granite and sandstone bulk took up the most prominent corner in town and dominated Main Street. There were forbidding steps leading up to its front door. Ordinary people didn't climb those steps very often, and they knew little about the mysteries inside. Most people got their wages in cash and paid their bills in cash or, sometimes, with money orders purchased at the post office—they didn't use the bank.

My father, who was then farming and trading in cattle, had to go to the bank regularly in order to finance his yearly operations or to raise money for a special project.

The bank president was a kindly and good man,

though severe, a deacon and usher in the First Baptist Church. His wife played the church piano, and his passable tenor voice could be heard all the way from the back pews, somehow rising above, in pitch and volume, the ordinary churchgoers' recitation of the doxology that marked the beginning of each service. Nobody thought it odd when he went to sleep during the sermons, or even considered it a matter worthy of comment. This seemed his due, a perquisite of his station.

And it seemed equally appropriate that the "Vagabonds," the most select local high school girls' club, required new pledges each year to scrub the bank steps with soap and water.

What I noted most about those early visits to the bank was that my father's tone and manner changed markedly when he entered the building. My father was—and is—a tough, independent, wiry, cowboy sort of person. Even when he had little else, he always had pride. When it was hard to buy groceries, he still had a good pair of cowboy boots built specially for him by the Olsen-Steltzer Boot Company of Henrietta, Texas. He always had a good Stetson hat. And most times, even when we lived in town and had no great use for one, he kept a high-quality horse.

He spent a lot of time in those days standing around at a particular drugstore corner, with other men dressed like himself, discussing cattle prices, forming transitory partnerships to make speculative purchases of cattle for shipping to Oklahoma City or Fort Worth, talking politics, telling jokes, and cussing the "interests."

He and his peers were men of honor, and in their circles the best that could be said of anyone was that his word was as good as his bond. My father was that kind of man. And men like him often said, "I wear no man's collar." He caused a sensation once in our town of Walters by calling a hardware dealer out of his store and slapping him in the face (the man was older than my dad) for harassing him about what my father considered an unjust bill. My father was immediately arrested and made to pay a fine of ten dollars and costs. Ten minutes later, he called the offending businessman out on the streets and slapped him again. "I'd pay ten dollars anytime for that kind of satisfaction," he said.

But he was a different man, it seemed to me, when he went to the bank. He took his hat off the minute he walked through the door. He waited his turn. When he was called through the swinging doors of the waist-high oak bar, my father stood at the banker's desk until he was asked to sit. His manner was deferential. He laid out his plans in supplicating tones. It might have been that he needed money to buy fifty head of stocker calves to feed out.

When my father was able to make a deal for a loan, he was grateful—very grateful. He said thank you, put his hat on, and went back on the street—where he was in control again, independent. The banker obviously felt good about his work, like a missionary doing the Lord's will. He'd encouraged another citizen, again, to reverence rectitude, self-sufficiency, and hard work.

I was long since grown before I learned that the banker didn't own the bank or any part of it. He was, himself, a tenant at sufferance, holding his position only so long as the absentee bankowner annually invested him with the feudal power he exercised in the hierarchical system that the bank really amounted to.

My other recollection has to do with a childhood saying we always chanted when we saw a shooting star outside at night. Playing games or sleeping outside, as we often did in those hot summer nights in Oklahoma before air conditioning, we felt almost surrounded by stars. On clear nights they were close enough to touch, and they covered every inch of the sky. Often a falling star would streak across the night ceiling, a mystery. Where did it come from, and where was it going? Why didn't it hit one of the millions of other, stationary shining lights? Whatever the explanations, a shooting star always made us say, as quickly as possible, "Money, money, money." You had to say it before anyone else could, and you had to say "money" all three times before the falling star disappeared. It brought good luck. Money.

We didn't know it then, but that was probably as good a way, as effective a magic, as any other for getting money, if one didn't already have it.

The situation's worse today. And not just in Walters, Oklahoma. A few large banks and insurance companies control the money and the economy of the entire country.

Banks have unique privileges as a special kind of business enterprise, supposedly not involved in other types of commercial and industrial activity. They control 75 percent of America's money supply. They're the only business corporations that by law have the privilege of receiving deposits for checking accounts without having to pay interest to the depositors for the use of such money.

Banks also get special tax treatment under federal law. For example, they are allowed to deduct for federal income tax purposes so-called bad-debt reserves, despite the fact that actual bad debts generally amount to only about one-sixth of the deductible reserve.

The central bank in the United States is the Federal Reserve. Even though it is federally chartered and its governors are appointed by the President, it is not a government bank but is privately owned. Neither is it controlled by government policy. It can, with little regard for official government policy, speed up or slow down the growth of the total money supply in the United States. And its decisions greatly affect the interest rates that ordinary borrowers have to pay.

In an expanding American economy, the Federal Reserve's policy of regularly expanding the money supply provides banks with a built-in growth and profitability. Bank profit margins have been diminishing, but their profits have increased because of growth—growth in the money supply and, more importantly for the banks, growth in their deposits and loans because of the growth and expansion of their commercial and industrial customers.

Banks, early on, moved beyond normal commercial banking activities—administering deposits and making loans. They also, through trust departments, manage trust estates and pension funds. By this means they hold and vote common stock in other corporations.

Insurance companies have a similar status, unique and protected. Formed for the purpose of providing a wider sharing of risks, insurance companies have become huge investors. And they too enjoy special federal and state tax privileges on the investment of funds that they control.

From the very first, it was recognized that these two special types of business enterprises—banks and insurance companies—could, unless restricted, wield enormous economic and political power. But regulation has been largely aimed toward protecting depositors and policyholders. Insurance companies are mostly regulated at the state level. Some banks are controlled at the state level, and all of them are regulated in a fragmented way by various federal agencies. Little attention at any level or by any agency has been given to curbing the growing economic power of banks and insurance companies.

Banks and insurance companies have therefore been able to restrict competition in their lucrative, protected, and privileged fields. Between 1950 and 1965 there were 2,200 bank mergers. There are now 13,000 commercial banks, but a mere 100 banks hold one-half of all bank deposits in the United States. One-fourth of all bank deposits are held by just 10 banks. And the 3 largest banks hold 13 percent of all deposits.

Regionally and locally, concentration is also the rule. In one-half of the states, five banks control one-half of all banking deposits in the state. In California, one bank alone controls nearly one-half of all deposits.

The same is true in regard to the banks' trust departments. The fifty largest bank trust departments control two-thirds of the $330 billion total bank trust department assets in America. Seventy percent of all U.S. pension funds are held by bank trust departments. Banks control 60 percent of all institutional investment in the American economy.

It's the same with insurance companies. The ten biggest life insurance companies control $130 billion in assets. That's more than one-half the assets of all life insurance companies in America.

The enormous economic power of the big banks and insurance companies is pyramided by their interlocking directorates. The ten largest life insurance companies and the ten largest commercial banks have 30 directors who are the same. The huge First National City Bank in New York has directors in common with six other banks and with twenty-one insurance companies. Forty-nine major American banks share 146 interlocking directorates with twenty-nine of the nation's largest insurance companies.

Theoretically, the ordinary borrower should be able to shop around for money and bargain on interest rates. But through the great number of mergers and acquisitions that the government has permitted, big banks and big insurance companies have been able to restrict competition and become even bigger. They've further reduced competition between banks and insurance companies by interlocking directorates.

And competition is reduced even further when the banks and insurance companies join forces with industrial companies. Forty-nine major American banks share 8,000 interlocking directors with 6,500 industrial companies—and most of these interlocking relationships link the largest U.S. banks and the largest U.S. industrial companies. For example, the First National City Bank in New York shares interlocking directors with forty of the largest American industrial corporations.

What this means is that the enormous lending power of the big banks is extended even further. It amounts to virtual control of American industry.

It also means that certain major industrial borrowers, connected with the banks, get preferential treatment that is not available to ordinary borrowers.

This intermingling of lending and industrial power is all-pervasive in America. The membership of the board of directors of Chase Manhattan Bank, for example, includes officers from all three vital U.S. industries—steel, automobiles, and oil.

Little wonder that banks pay scant attention to loans for low-income housing, say. Little wonder that states and cities, even though their bonds are tax-exempt, are required to pay interest rates that are only 30 percent lower than corporate borrowing costs.

The evils of interlocking directorates include suppression of competition between supposedly competing industrial companies. It is highly unlikely that Continental Illinois National Bank and Trust is going to loan money to Union Oil for the purpose of making it more competitive with Standard Oil of Indiana and Universal Oil, because all three oil companies are represented on the bank's board of directors. Morgan Guaranty Trust is not going to assist Continental Oil toward greater competition with Atlantic Richfield or Exxon. They're all represented on Morgan's board, as are both U.S. Steel and Bethlehem Steel and both General Motors and Ford.

If the ordinary borrower is to have any power in the borrowing marketplace, the government must do its duty and reverse mergers and acquisitions between financial institutions, breaking up the big banks and the big insurance companies. It must act to end the incestuous interlocking relationship between types of financial institutions. And it must eliminate their interlocking relationships with industrial corporations.

The government must act, too, to prevent financial institutions, enjoying special, protected legal and tax status, from using their economic power to engage in and control other types of business and industrial activity. Otherwise, as the Economics Division of the Federal Trade Commission predicted some years ago, "All major economic decisions in the United States may be made by less than 200 persons within a decade."

Banks are, theoretically, prevented from taking a share in ownership and control of the enterprises to which they supply money. But they have found ways around this restriction.

One way is through their trust departments, which are supposed to be separate from regular banking operations. An industrial company quickly understands that it has a better chance to get a loan if the industrial company's pension fund management is given to the lending bank's trust department. Bank trust departments regularly vote common stock owned by pension funds that they control in accordance with the wishes of the management of a particular industrial company—if the industrial company's management is doing banking and trust department business with the bank.

So it is that a great many industrial companies that are said to be "management-operated" are companies in which commercial banks, through their trust departments, own a significant part of the common stock of the company.

Morgan Guaranty's trust department, for example, controls more than 16 percent of the commercial stock of Burlington Industries, nearly 16 percent of Disney Productions, 10 percent of Masonite, nearly 9 percent of Polaroid, more than 8 percent of Squibb, 8 percent of Avon Products, nearly 6 percent of U.S. Plywood, 5.5 percent of Xerox, and 5 percent of Westinghouse.

The trust department of First National City Bank controls 7.5 percent of Phillips Petroleum, more than 7.5 percent of Texas Industries, 9 percent of Bendix Corporation, nearly 6 percent of TRW, Inc., and nearly 6 percent of Xerox.

Banks and their trust departments should be totally separated by law and made to operate separately and independently as the law originally intended.

Banks also use what's called the "equity kicker" to get around the legal prohibition against being involved in industrial ownership. Ordinary borrowers, who cannot or will not give up a share of ownership in order to borrow money, are discriminated against. The equity kicker mostly comes into play with "growth" industries that are hard up for cash. The bank lends money for expansion. But it wants more than just the interest on the lent money. The law prohibits it from taking stock ownership. So it takes stock warrants—the right to buy stock in the future at a pegged price. When the stock goes up in value, the bank, which can't convert the warrant to actual stock, nevertheless can sell the warrant, making a profit over and above the interest on the money it has lent. And federal tax laws allow the bank to get special tax treatment on this profit by means of the capital gains loophole.

Some banks do the same thing another way—by indirection. They take the equity kicker in future cash, pegged to an increase in the price of the stock of the borrowing company. For example, when First National City Bank loaned $25 million to City Investing to buy Rheem Manufacturing Company, the bank required, over and above the interest on the loan, an agreement that City Investing would pay the bank $50,000 for every point that City Investing's stock went up in its market price. By this method alone, First National City Bank also made a quarter of a million dollars, in addition to the interest it earned, when the bank loaned Stirling Homex the money to go public.

This kind of sharing by banks in the benefits of ownership in enterprises to which they have loaned money ought to be prohibited by law, if it isn't already.

But the best device banks have found to get around the law that prohibits their involvement in other commercial and industrial businesses, is the one-bank holding company. The bank forms a parent company, with the same directors and owners, which controls the bank and other enterprises also. By this means banks have moved into insurance, travel service, leasing, data processing, mutual funds, and other activities.

These related enterprises obviously have better borrowing ability at the bank than unrelated businesses. The banks thus use their special tax and other legal privileges to compete unfairly with other enterprises that are not bank-owned. Between 1955 and 1968 bank holding companies increased sevenfold. Most of the largest banks have made use of this way around the law.

By forming a holding company, a bank can restrict the voting power of minority stockholders in the bank, expand into geographic areas from which the bank is otherwise barred, and gain greater tax advantages. Recent legislation passed by Congress to close these loopholes in the law was so watered down that the law actually encourages banks to use the holding company device in the future. The law pretty much sanctions past bank holding company operations.

Banks should either be banks or they should be another kind of business or industrial corporation. They shouldn't be allowed to use the special incentives they enjoy to compete unfairly with other enterprises. Holding companies should not be allowed at all.

Bigness in banks begets bigness in industry. This works in two ways. First, industries are encouraged to become bigger because of the banks' practice of loaning money to their big customers at "prime" rates—interest rates lower than smaller borrowers have to pay. More important, big banks use their economic power actually to encourage mergers and acquisitions by their borrowers. Aside from purely financial considerations, Chase Manhattan was willing to loan Gulf + Western, a conglomerate, huge sums to buy other firms because the purchased companies would themselves become Chase Manhattan customers. That could be why First National City Bank financed Kennecott Copper's acquisition of Peabody Coal, Continental Oil's acquisition of Consolidation Coal, Atlantic Richfield's acquisition of Sinclair Oil, and Hess Oil's acquisition of Amerada.

When Teledyne, Inc., a customer of First National City

Bank of New York, bought the Monarch Rubber Company, the First National Bank of Canton, Ohio, lost most of Monarch's deposits to First National City, and the Harder Bank and Trust Company of Canton lost Monarch's $2.5 million pension fund to First National City's trust department. And so financial control was further removed from the people, further centralized in New York City.

The big banks financed the mergers that gave birth to the Penn Central and Lockheed, not because of the profitability of the loans, but because of this same desire for growth in bank business. The big banks themselves created these awkward behemoths. But when the merged industries threatened to topple because of their own weight, the big banks told Congress that unless the federal taxpayers bailed the banks out, preventing the bankruptcy of the merged companies, the whole economy of the country would suffer because Lockheed and the Penn Central were so big. And the government has generally agreed to such blackmail, although the agreement amounts to a reverse incentive for future giant-building, through more bank-financed mergers and acquisitions. Unless stopped, banks will go right on, Congressman William Moorehead of Pennsylvania says, creating dinosaurs that one day show up at our door saying, "If you don't feed me, I will die"—the alternative being a dead, ten-ton carcass stinking up our front steps.

Free enterprise means nothing unless it means freedom to fail, as well as freedom to succeed. In the Soviet Union, which doesn't even operate on the free enterprise system, anyone who managed or financed such inefficient failures as Lockheed and the Penn Central would have to suffer the consequences. In our country, we have rewarded such mismanagers with a taxpayer bail-out, which mostly benefits the big banks.

There is another evil of concentrated financial power. Big banks are able to circumvent and avoid the effects of national monetary policy. In times of inflation the Federal Reserve usually slows the growth in money supply; in times of recession it usually expands the money supply. The Federal Reserve does this by varying its loan requirements for member banks and by altering its regulations concerning financial reserves that member banks must hold. But the banks use commercial paper issued by their foreign subsidiaries or their bank holding companies to create new money, in effect, even though the Federal Reserve has acted to tighten up on the national money supply.

I have long felt that the whole system of expanding or slowing the growth of money, nationwide, doesn't work. The banks, even when money is tight, still continue to take care of their biggest and best customers—at a better rate than ordinary borrowers can command, if they can get loans at all. And social goals, such as the need for increased housing, generally suffer most.

More fundamentally, I've always thought it odd that the central bank that makes these decisions, the Federal Reserve, is privately owned and is not subject to direct public control. The Bank of England, on the other hand, is subject to government policy.

Every study—the most recent and best having been done by the House Banking and Currency Committee, chaired by Congressman Wright Patman of Texas, shows that most academic and financial experts think the American central banking system, where private interests make what are, in fact, public decisions, is crazy. But most recommendations for change in the system tend to center around more and better government regulation.

The New Populism maintains that the basic problem is that the Federal Reserve is privately owned. The

House Banking and Currency Committee has clearly shown that commercial banks control the selection of Federal Reserve directors. The banks, in effect, choose the officials who will decide upon the supply of money and the level of interest rates—and they look after their own interests.

The New Populism holds that faith in government regulation of a private monopoly is largely misplaced faith. The Federal Reserve controls America's money supply. It is a natural monopoly, and it has overriding power in the money marketplace. The only way to protect the public interest is by public ownership.

Congressman John R. Rarick of Louisiana has introduced a bill in the House of Representatives to provide for the purchase of Federal Reserve stock by the government. Congressman Rarick is a conservative. But this is neither a conservative nor a liberal issue. It is a question of whether the people will have fuller power over their own lives.

There's no reason why private banks ought to be given a special franchise to earn extra profits through high interest rates for doing what is supposedly a public-spirited act—that is, raising interest rates and tightening up on the money supply to hold down inflation. Yet that is the present situation. Congressman Rarick is right in seeking to change it.

Drive around any town or city in America, and you'll see that the newest and best buildings are the banks. They're doing well. They do just as well in bad times as in good. That's because we all have to have money—and hiring out money is what banks do.

While they are turning their money into more money, using their economic power to gain more economic power, most of the rest of the people struggle just to get along and feed their families.

The New Populism

When I was growing up, my mother always said that being poor was no disgrace. But even then I was more inclined to agree with humorist Frank McKinney, who once said, "It's no disgrace to be poor, but it might as well be."

Even then, too, I noted that Horatio Alger stories, while seeming to idealize the go-getter, actually depicted heroes who *lucked* into money all at once—by saving a rich man's daughter, for instance. Ours ought to be an economic system that rewards hard work and initiative. In spite of everything, it isn't.

When F. Scott Fitzgerald said, "The rich are different from us," Ernest Hemingway was reported to have responded, "Yes, they have more money." Today fewer and fewer of us have a chance to be "different," even in a small degree.

Our country started out to be one where the big banks and the big insurance companies didn't control all the money, where ordinary people had a real chance to get some money. We can be that kind of country again.

CHAPTER

VIII

End the Greenbacking of America

In early 1972 I visited a number of counties in West Virginia, Kentucky, and Tennessee to learn more, firsthand, about strip-mining, and what can be done about it. Friends who live in those counties drove me along the country backroads. We slogged up and down hills that had been scraped off by bulldozers and made sterile. I walked with them along murky, muddy streams ruined by strip-mining.

Later in the year I sponsored a national conference on strip-mining in Hazard, Kentucky. People came from twelve states at their own expense. They made clear that what I had seen myself in one area of the United States had already spread all over the country—and that it was continuing to spread.

Campbell County, Tennessee, is a typical example. Although it has great riches in natural resources, Campbell County is home to some of the poorest people in

America. Economically, it falls in the bottom 10 percent of U.S. counties. And yet Campbell County contains some of the most beautiful valleys and streams anywhere in the world. But the thick timber is being shoved down the hillsides so that the strip miners can get to the buried coal seams. Rains cause acids to leach out of the uncovered earth, poisoning the streams below. Erosion fills up the stream beds with run-off mud. The natural habitat of wildlife is destroyed, and fish are killed by sediment and acid pollution.

I talked with the people. I ate in their homes. I listened to what they had to say. Standing on their front porches, I saw hills that had once been richly forested but now reminded me of the bare Badlands of South Dakota where nothing grows. I saw country roads barricaded by impassable rockslides. I visited homes where the waters from flash floods caused by silted-in creek beds had left ankle-deep muck on the floors and muddy couches and curtains that couldn't be cleaned.

What the mother and the grandmother of a young man who had died in the last flood told me made it clear that their fear of new floods was not just theoretical.

I talked with mine union officials who had seen their own workers put out of jobs by the huge strip-mining machines. I went with them to strip-mine sites and saw, close up, the incredible damage being done for what are really small seams of coal.

I walked along a stream with an old deep-miner who said he had fished for small-mouth bass and other game fish in that very creek five or six years before. Now, because of leached acids seeping down from the naked hills, the stream is dead. No living thing can exist in it. I visited homes that had been jarred and faulted for months by the huge strip-mine explosive charges nearby.

I was shocked that this kind of permanent injury could

be inflicted on people and the land and the streams—injury committed with impunity—in the last third of the twentieth century in America.

But don't think that I talked with just the one side. I also met with representatives of the large landholders and the strip miners. They couldn't offer any defense for their actions. They admitted that the slopes cannot be restored to their natural condition—or anything near it. They were unable to direct me to even one strip-mine operation where reclamation has taken place. The topsoil torn off by these hillside strip-mining operations has gone down the slopes, most often destroying the streams below. The topsoil cannot be reclaimed or put back. The silted stream beds—some completely covered up now—cannot be repaired. The trees and fish killed by acids are gone forever. And what was once level ground in strip-mined valleys now looks like mountains on the moon.

Neither did the large landholders and strip miners have any defense to the charge that they pay only a small percentage of their fair share of local taxes. They pay no severance tax on the mined coal. Their land is assessed for taxation at absurdly low values. And mining equipment is not assessed at all.

Much of the land in Campbell County—and other strip-mine counties—is owned by out-of-state interests. Some of it—particularly the acreage owned by a British corporation, which is, interestingly enough, known as the American Association—is foreign-owned. Because of these large landholdings, some communities can't even get a little bit of land for a school building. Other towns are denied land for a housing project. "The only thing wrong with these hills," one manager of a large land company has said, "is the people." The strip miners and large landholders do not want to be bothered by people. They are pushing them off the land as rapidly as they can.

The New Populism

The late Senator George Norris of Nebraska, and all other original sponsors of legislation creating the Tennessee Valley Authority, would be saddened if they were alive today. Flood control and conservation were among the fundamental concepts of TVA. Yet, today, in order to buy cheap coal for its steam-generator plants, TVA is the principal purchaser of strip-mined coal. Some of its own lands are being strip-mined. TVA policies are ruining streams, destroying forest environment, increasing the incidence of floods, and exploiting powerless people—the kinds of things TVA was set up to prevent.

The state regulation of strip-mining has actually amounted to a license to continue the worst practices. And in 1972 a strip-mining bill reported out of a U.S. Senate committee was correctly judged by environmental groups to be worse than no bill at all.

How do the strip miners get away with it? They get away with it because economic power translates into political power.

There are plenty of other examples. The people of Oklahoma, for one, are having to pay millions of dollars too much for medicines because of the political power of the major drug companies. Oklahoma and a great many other states have what's called an "antisubstitution" law.

The original intent of the law was fine. A pharmacist was to be prohibited from substituting one generic drug for another. If a doctor prescribed tetracycline hydrochloride, an antibiotic, the pharmacist could not substitute penicillin, another antibiotic, when he filled the prescription. The reason was that a good many people are allergic to penicillin. So the law was quite right in prohibiting the substitution of one type of drug for another, one generic drug for another.

But that's not the problem. The problem for Okla-

161

homa consumers comes about because there are a good many manufacturers of the same identical drugs, and because drug manufacturers have been allowed to twist the original law to their advantage.

Owing to intense lobbying efforts by the National Pharmaceutical Council—made up of the largest trade-name drug manufacturers—a totally different interpretation of the antisubstitution law has been adopted in Oklahoma and in many other states. Under this new interpretation, a local druggist is prohibited from substituting one *brand* for another brand, even though the drug is identically—generically—the same, and all the drugs are standardized and approved by the U.S. Food and Drug Administration.

Here's how this particular system works. If in prescribing tetracycline hydrochloride a doctor writes on the prescription "Achromycin-V," which is Lederle's brand name for that drug, the Oklahoma pharmacist is prohibited from filling the prescription with "Panmycin," which is Upjohn's brand name for the same antibiotic. The druggist is prohibited from making this substitution, even though the drugs are identical and one is much cheaper than the other.

This scandalous exploitation of Oklahoma people who have to buy medicines means that in general they have to pay far too much for medicine. Or, what's worse, for people of limited income, it means that they may not be able to buy needed medicine at all. Oklahomans are paying $1.5 million too much annually on only eight often-prescribed drugs.

A majority of Oklahoma pharmacists don't like this system, and they would substitute identical lower-priced drugs for brand names if they were allowed to do so. This is also the position of the National Association of Retail Druggists. Under the antisubstitution law, a pharmacist has to stock a large inventory—sometimes as many as ten different brand names—in every particular drug, because he isn't allowed to substitute.

Opponents of this law in Oklahoma have not been able even to get the state legislature to hold hearings on it. And more and more states around the country are adopting similarly restrictive interpretations of the original antisubstitution law.

This is just one of the examples of how monopolistic drug companies flex their political muscles. Nationally, by this means and others, they are allowed to overcharge consumers by 30 percent—about $2.1 billion annually.

Another example of how economic power becomes political power: the big insurance companies and the trial lawyers have been able to stymie congressional efforts to enact a no-fault insurance law that would cut automobile insurance costs drastically. Big industry has teamed up to sidetrack a tough new consumer protection law.

When new regulatory laws are passed, more often than not, those who are supposed to be regulated wind up controlling the regulators. President Nixon's wage and price control officials were recently forced to admit that prices shot up more during the first year of controls than they did in the year before controls went into effect.

Economic power should be broken up because of its devastating economic impact, its subversion of the natural economic pressures. But even aside from this obvious point, there is reason enough for breaking up concentrated economic power in order to decrease its political control.

Political reforms and increased government regulation, however well intended, have no chance of really changing things so long as inordinate economic concentration continues unchecked.

Economic power becomes political power in a number of obvious ways: through tax-exempt lobbying and advertising; through corporate involvement in community affairs; through job interchange between government and industry.

And, by one of the most invidious routes, concentrated wealth and economic power become political power through the financing of political campaigns.

The summer I graduated from law school, I became involved in the unsuccessful campaign of Roy J. Turner to unseat the incumbent United States senator from Oklahoma, Robert S. Kerr.

Both Kerr and Turner were oil millionaires. As the impending clash between these colossi of roads (asphalt) grew more apparent and ineluctable, observers could foresee, correctly, the greenbacking, if not the greening, of Oklahoma in the campaign days ahead.

The sharp guys came out in coveys, as they would in any state. Some wanted to be county or town campaign manager for whichever candidate would pay the most. An unprincipled preacher offered to bargain away his influence with his unsuspecting congregation. A door-to-door cosmetics saleswoman was willing to consider—for a price—adding a pitch for a candidate to her usual sales promotion to regular-route customers.

And there were the ubiquitous importunings of hundreds of poll haulers and hangers-on. These people wanted everything from $25,000 to carry a county to a half pint of whiskey to "make the day"—from fifty dollars for "gas and expenses" to get to the district church conference, to a thousand dollars to pay back taxes to keep a weekly newspaper operating. Most were turned away.

One young man in the Turner headquarters had as his principal duty to run to a nearby bank every day as soon as it opened to bring back a thousand or so dollars in cash to be doled out to those who came in declaring that victory in their counties would require a little money "to put on a barbecue" or "to hire some women to pick up old folks on Election Day." The great old political wizard who managed the Turner campaign, H. W. "Coach" McNeil, would call the young man into his office each morning and hand him a draft to be cashed at the bank. "My boy," he would say every time with solemn and ritualistic regularity, "we're a little short on frog hair." And just as regularly as the scarce "frog hair" came back from the bank in the form of crisp new bills, it was regularly dispensed by the Coach before the sun went down.

That was in 1954; a lot of oil has gone under the bridge since then. Ironically, Turner, as rich as he was, had to pull out of the race because he ran out of money. Robert Kerr went back to the Senate.

Ten years later, I ran myself, successfully, for the United States Senate from Oklahoma. By then the big money went into television, rather than influence payments. But the overall campaign costs had actually increased.

I was able to win without the small payments of the earlier political era because of the good advice I got on free news publicity and paid television. I even won in Muskogee, the home of my principal Democratic opponent, Senator J. Howard Edmondson, without having spent a *traditional* dime—a fact that damn near destroyed the already ailing system of paid politics.

In getting elected to the Senate in 1964, I raised money in three stages: bluffing plus personal loans; bluffing plus big first contributions; and bluffing plus a lot of small contributions.

Ultimately, most of the money came from a lot of small contributors. And I am told now by friends and others involved that the entire campaign cost around $750,000.

The campaign involved a tough Democratic primary and runoff with former governor Raymond Gary and former governor and incumbent Senator Edmondson, as well as an arduous general election contest with the famous Oklahoma football coach Charles B. "Bud" Wilkinson.

It seems incredible that I could have spent that much. I remember only the deadlines, the daily crises. "WKY-TV is going to release the television spots they have allotted to you at four o'clock this afternoon unless you can come up with $4,500." "The billboard people have to have $3,200 in the morning or they're going to sell the space to Wilkinson." "We can't get our new bumper stickers from the printers unless we can come up with $2,000 by noon." It was a daily and sometimes hourly scramble.

I borrowed the beginning money on my personal note at the Security Bank and Trust Company of Lawton, Oklahoma. This was three thousand dollars, later increased to six thousand. And we bluffed a lot. The press and the pros will not take you seriously unless they think you have the money. It doesn't matter what you're saying or what kind of candidate you are. If you don't have the money, they figure you're not going anywhere. So why should they bother with you? My friends and supporters put out the word that the financial situation was better than we had ever expected. The press wrote me up as a serious contender. And the pros read the press.

Next came the first big money. When it's time to spend money—to buy advertising, to hire staff, to open an office—you either have it or you don't.

A lot of old-time Oklahoma farmers still won't plant potatoes, say, unless the signs—astrological signs and the phase of the moon—are right. In campaigns, not many people will give you money or write in a newspaper that you have a chance unless the signs are right. But they aren't looking at the moon—the right signs are there when you seem to have the money.

I spent a great deal of my own time soliciting big contributors. Some of these were people who liked me and what I said, and they hoped I'd win. Most of them were people who disliked Raymond Gary or Howard Edmondson or Bud Wilkinson and thought I presented the best chance of beating the candidate they most disliked. A few of them were afraid I might win and decided to put a little money on me for insurance.

We parlayed these contributions into a winning campaign. We puffed them up and trumpeted them about. We waved our checks around and dropped every name that would make a thud. And press people and pros began to write and say, "You know, this young Harris may surprise a lot of people." That's all you need. It is not necessary that the opinion molders write or say that you will be a winner. It *is* necessary that they say you *can* be a winner.

Finally we had raised enough initial money to come to the attention of my natural constituents. And, most important, we had special coffee-schools for hundreds of people who volunteered to help, to convince them that they themselves could be opinion molders if they were willing to speak out without fear of ridicule for supporting me, and we gave them the skills to speak with confidence. Advertising we saw as a means of identifying and reinforcing supporters.

Essentially, I won the 1964 Senate race by being able to identify and enlist the vigorous support of thousands of volunteers. The last money and the biggest sum, as well as work, came from them. But the crucial financial stage was soliciting successfully the few first big contributors. It only takes a few of them, but this was the stage where I fell down in my short-lived presidential campaign in 1971.

Fred R. Harris

The question is: how do you harvest frog hair without getting warts?

Between July, 1971, when I decided to run for the Democratic nomination for President, and November, when I announced I was having to close down because I was broke and $40,000 in the hole, I spent $200,000.

About a third of that amount was raised in relatively small contributions (around $100 each) from a great many friends in Oklahoma. About a third of it came from friends and supporters in Los Angeles, Miami, and elsewhere in the country, people I had come to know when I was chairman of the Democratic National Committee. The most crucial—and initial—third of the money came from the personal contributions and solicitations of Herbert A. Allen, Jr., a brilliant young New York investment banker who had got involved in politics during the 1968 presidential campaign, primarily because of his interest in ending the war in Vietnam.

Most people cannot conceive of how costly campaigns are. In the 1970 Senate campaigns, eleven of the fifteen major candidates in the seven biggest states were millionaires. The four who were not millionaires lost.

Nelson Rockefeller spent $10 million getting reelected governor of New York in 1970, and John Lindsay spent $3 million in his campaign for reelection as mayor of New York City. John Tower reported expenditures of $2.5 million for his 1972 Senate reelection campaign in Texas.

The presidential campaigns of 1968 *reported* expenditures of $44.2 million. The 1972 campaigns cost even more.

I ran for President in 1971 because I believed people want—and are entitled to have—fundamental changes in their lives and in their society. People feel powerless, and they despair that the political process can change much, because there is too great a concentration of political and economic power in too few hands.

I wanted to see measures to put an end to unfair tax loopholes. I believed that a realization of America's promise and ideals required these measures and other fundamental and structural changes to bring about a more equitable distribution of wealth, income, and power.

You might imagine that the doctrines of the New Populism went down a little better in union halls, college auditoriums, old folks' homes, and minority rallies than they did at fund-raising luncheons at the 21 Club.

Somehow, I tended to get more radical when I spoke to a rich group. And there were always some people who were willing to bet a little on a candidate who told the truth about the need to try to make the system work and help America live up to what we always said it was. Often my hosts at fund-raising sessions were disappointed, however, that I wasn't a little less candid about what I planned to do if I were elected President. "You lost so-and-so when you mentioned you were against the business investment tax credit."

One of my principal backers (not Allen) became increasingly alienated by my talk about breaking up shared monopolies. "Couldn't he just stick to the dope traffic and safe subjects like that?" he asked my campaign manager.

The worst thing I could say was any talk about the capital gains provisions of the tax laws, which are particularly lucrative for Wall Street brokers. Liberals don't get much money from the oil industry, and it's therefore not too difficult to talk of doing something about the oil depletion allowance. But liberals get a lot of money from Wall Street. Joseph Duffey, the former president of

Americans for Democratic Action who ran for the United States Senate from Connecticut in 1970, chilled some of his best contributors to the point of freezing their pocketbooks when he included the capital gains tax in his list of the tax reforms that are needed.

Americans, at least in principle, would never agree to the rule of primogeniture for determining who will exercise political power. Nor would we agree in principle to the "one dollar, one vote" political system that oil-rich reactionary H. L. Hunt once advocated in a self-promoting novel he wrote.

Yet consider that the Mellon family gave nearly a quarter of a million dollars to the national Republican party in 1968 and nearly a million in 1972, that Nelson Rockefeller and one sister gave over $100,000 in 1968, and that the Pew family of Philadelphia gave nearly $200,000. One thing these families have in common is that their inherited fortunes depend to a large extent on oil interests. In 1968 members of the National Petroleum Council gave the Nixon campaign more than $100,000 and more still in 1972. These contributions may not be unrelated to President Nixon's veto of his own task force's recommendation that the protective oil import quota system be scrapped in favor of a more competitive tariff system. One man, one vote? The overcharged customers in fuel-hungry New England would probably say it isn't so.

Insurance executive W. Clement Stone of Chicago, who gave the Nixon campaign $500,000 in 1968 and $1 million in 1972, and who contributed around $1 million to various GOP candidates in 1970, was asked about the size of his contributions. He responded, "If a family has wealth in the neighborhood of $400 million, what's a million in gifts?"

Maybe not much to Mr. Stone. But that much money

is quite a lot to a man who has only one vote. And it's no easier for the average person to take when he sees that he pays more than his share of taxes—while a lot of rich men like Mr. Stone do not—and yet he can't afford essential things like medical care.

When Common Cause insisted that he name his financial backers, Mr. Nixon made a partial disclosure of the rich people who had largely financed his 1972 campaign. Oil-rich J. Paul Getty was listed at $50,000, a figure so low under the circumstances that an automobile worker in Flint, Michigan, told me, "He tricked Dick; anybody who can avoid $70 million a year in federal income taxes and only makes a political contribution of $50,000 is getting off too cheap."

It is not just a matter of whether one agrees or disagrees with the political philosophy of the big contributors. Consider Stewart Mott, a thirty-five-year-old bachelor who lives in Manhattan and cultivates an extensive penthouse vegetable and flower garden. Mr. Mott is a political philanthropist whose second hobby, next to gardening, is giving money to politicians who agree with his views in favor of peace and population control, or who will change their views to suit him. During a ten-week period in 1968, he publicly pledged $50,000 each to the presidential campaigns of Nelson Rockefeller and Eugene McCarthy. He wound up that year making political contributions, mostly to McCarthy, totaling $365,000. And he was a huge contributor to the 1972 McGovern campaign.

My farmer father is a better gardener than Mr. Mott. He doesn't go to bed each night worrying about the best way to plant things so much as he does about whether they'll be worth anything after they come up. Presidential candidates do not, as a rule, line up to ask my father his views on national and international affairs. That may be one reason that so many small farmers like him are being pushed off the land by the rich and corporation farmers who receive huge tax and farm payments subsidies. People with money, like Mr. Mott, can get a senator on the telephone. My father can't.

President Harry S. Truman came to Oklahoma City during his uphill 1948 reelection campaign. After a personal appearance and a national radio speech, he was told by railroad officials that they would not move his campaign train unless he came up with a sizable cash payment. Even though he was President, and despite the humiliation, he scraped the money together with a lot of urgent late-night telephone calls.

I couldn't get *my* train moving again in November, 1971—just when the populist constituency was beginning to be stirred.

The Washington Post columnist David Broder wrote on November 16, 1971, after I withdrew from the presidential campaign: "Harris quit because he was flat broke, and the prospects for raising money to back a 'populist' candidate who proposed to talk in blunt terms about the maldistribution of wealth and income and taxes in America were nil."

He wrote that had I been able to stay in the race, win or not, my campaign might have forced the other Democratic candidates—and even President Nixon—to respond to these issues.

Then Broder pointed out the contrast between the fate of my campaign and that of Senator Henry Jackson of Washington, who, he wrote, "has no more popular support for the presidency today than did Fred Harris. . . . What Jackson does have is a record that makes him very popular with a certain few people . . . who happen to have money to spend on politics. Whatever happens to Jackson's candidacy, the Democratic nominee will have to respond to those [Jackson's] issues, but not Harris's issues because Jackson, not Harris, is the kind of candidate who can raise the money to run a campaign."

I came out of my brief presidential campaign with renewed determination to reform campaign financing. Stiffer disclosure laws and tightened controls on how much money can be spent will help, as will the new law that gives tax credits for smaller campaign contributions. It would help, too, if nominees for the Congress, the Senate, and the Presidency were guaranteed a minimum amount of television time at reduced cost.

But these are just reforms. They do not attack the fundamental problem—concentrated economic power. Senator George McGovern's invaluable and coveted list of 600,000 small contributors to his 1972 presidential campaign is a strong indication that it might be possible, over time and with considerable effort, to put together a campaign for public office that would not be prevented in advance, because of how it had raised its money, from attacking economic concentration.

Concentrated economic power also uses tax-exempt lobbying and advertising to protect its privileges. Consider automobile safety. At the beginning of 1971, the National Highway Safety Bureau recommended that airbags be required on all cars manufactured after April, 1973. This recommendation came from extensive tests finding that a reliable airbag device, designed for split-second inflation after impact, would save as many as 24,000 lives a year—lives now lost in automobile accidents.

Ford disagreed with the recommendation—for financial reasons—and it undertook to "educate" the public. Like other shared monopoly companies, Ford normally spends enormous sums on advertising. The company regularly passes this advertising expense along to the consumer in the form of increased prices. It was easy, then, for Ford to pour hundreds of thousands of dollars into ads against airbags.

The net result of their campaign was that the date for requiring airbags was pushed back two years. Ford was able to build enough doubt about airbag effectiveness in the minds of the general public that federal administrators felt safe in bowing to Ford demands.

Steel companies have spent enormous sums in advertising to tell us about the joys and benefits of strip-mining. And oil companies, to hear them tell it, are among America's foremost environmentalists. Typical of their message was a two-page ad from Standard Oil of New Jersey that appeared in national magazines. It featured a picture of two small children walking on a deserted beach. The headline read, "What kind of world will we leave them?" Then the advertising copy boasted of a new process developed by Standard to clean oil tanker compartments at sea "that helps to eliminate putting any oil into the ocean." The ad concluded: "We intend to do what we can to improve the quality of life on this planet."

Praiseworthy rhetoric, to be sure. But in that same year, 1970 (according to testimony before the Marine Environmental Protection Division of the U.S. Coast Guard), a Standard tanker spilled 386,000 gallons of oil in Long Island Sound. It formed an oil slick sixteen miles long that washed ashore and closed municipal beaches. In the same year, another Standard tanker spilled 1.9 million gallons of crude oil off the coast of Nova Scotia. It cost $1.3 million to clean up that spill.

And that's not all. Another tanker from Standard's Humble division spilled 67,000 gallons of oil into the Chesapeake Bay in 1970. And, still in 1970, the Justice Department announced that a Standard company had refused to install safety devices on thirty-three of its offshore oil wells in the Gulf of Mexico.

In 1971 Texaco placed ads headlined: "Texaco prohibits the discharge of their oil into the sea—anywhere in the world." And that year they spilled 242,000 gallons of diesel oil in Puget Sound, contaminating seventeen miles of beach.

The following year, 1972, Texaco joined Standard and Atlantic Richfield in an even bigger advertising campaign—buying eleven pages of full-page color ads in one magazine alone, *Harper's,* to congratulate themselves on their fine environmental protection efforts.

What can be done to cut down this corporate brainwashing? Enforcement of the "fairness doctrine" will help, giving groups some semblance of equal access to the television advertising channels. More basically, the tax loophole that allows corporations to deduct such advertising on public questions from their federal income taxes should be closed.

President Nixon's 1972 reelection campaign featured a major exploitation of this tax loophole. His supporters, led by Hobart Lewis of *Reader's Digest* and William Marriott, the hotel and restaurant chain owner, set up "Citizens for a New Prosperity" to solicit tax-deductible contributions from corporations as "ordinary and necessary business expenses." They used these funds to buy full-page ads and to distribute newsletters and other propaganda aimed at convincing the American people that President Nixon's economic policies were working and were good for ordinary people, not just for big business.

Corporations can also deduct the cost of direct lobbying from their taxable income. In 1971 Hill and Knowlton, a public relations firm, was hired by the airline industry to lobby for legislation favorable to it. "We believe that the intention of the industry should be to build a pyramid of support reaching upward from a large base throughout the country to a pinnacle in Washington," the firm wrote in a memo to its clients. "At the top of the pinnacle is, of course, official Washington, including: members of the Senate and the House of Representatives and their aides; staff personnel of key committees of both Houses; members and staff of the Civil Aeronautics Board; appropriate officials and staff of the Department of Transportation and the Department of Labor; key White House staff personnel and executive agencies such as the Council of Economic Advisers and the Office of Management and Budget." What chance does the ordinary airline *passenger* have to express his wants in the face of this kind of effort?

Hill and Knowlton undertook, also, to put out a newsletter to a wide mailing list, and they recommended special efforts to influence a "few score academicians and others who are the most perspicacious minds behind the consumerist and environmentalist movements . . . the men who lead movements, write the rationale that others follow, testify before government committees and serve on commissions. . . . These men should be cultivated by airline executives individually and should receive the industry's position papers and newsletters. . . . The companies should give careful thought to means of bringing individuals from these groups into the association, perhaps through summer employment fellowships, or making contributions to college meeting-expenses funds—which are often insufficient to permit as much travel as academicians would like—or by retaining selected individuals as consultants."

It isn't just the airlines who use corporate power to secure their aims. Since 1958, when it illegally bought a competing gas pipeline company, El Paso Natural Gas Company has been in violation of the federal antitrust laws. Four times since that purchase, the United States

Supreme Court has ruled that El Paso Gas must divest itself of this illegal property. After El Paso had kept the matter in the courts for years—something ordinary taxpayers who don't have the money can't do—the gas company still didn't give up. They decided to ask the Congress for *retroactive* legislation to allow them to avoid complying with the law and decisions.

The company paid a New York public relations firm $1.7 million to help drum up public support for their case. "El Paso's ability to do this," Professor John Flynn of Utah, an antitrust expert, has said, "is derived in part from the ability of a regulated monopoly (interstate gas pipeline companies are regulated by the Federal Power Commission) to charge all company expenditures in the battle to the rate base. In a very real sense, the public has been bearing the real cost of El Paso's continued attempts to avoid compliance with the law, because the expense of the battle is dropped into the rate base."

El Paso has been able to marshal a wide array of witnesses to come before the Congress—where the bill is still pending—to show that customers of El Paso, ranging from gas distributors to local school systems, support their legislative position. But, as Professor Flynn again points out, this evidence is a direct result of the economic power of the company. "El Paso . . . has been diligently lobbying state officials, distributing companies, business groups and others in the West to support their position for the bill," he said. "Consequently there is an apparent uniformity of support for and no opposition to the El Paso position, and public officials in this part of the country have not had the opportunity to hear all sides of the case."

Because of its concentrated economic power, El Paso is able to hire the best lawyers, the best public relations firms, and the best economists. It has invested thousands of dollars in the cause of explaining its case to the public. Gas consumers have no such chance.

Neither do consumers or ordinary citizens have the opportunity to wine and dine government officials as the big corporations can. The Washington lobbyist T. H. Casey described his work, promoting the International Telephone & Telegraph Corporation's efforts to get space and defense contracts from the federal government, in these words: "In order to do this, it is necessary to have business and social contacts at the highest levels in the Department of Defense." Casey and his wife, he said, attend at least two receptions or dinners a week, representing ITT. In addition to this, they hold dinner parties and other affairs in their own home, regularly throughout each month.

Casey's boss at ITT, William Merriam, is a member of the Carlton Club, an exclusive gathering place for top Washington lobbyists. The Carlton's forty members also include Procter & Gamble's lobbyist Bryce Harlow, Ford's Rod Markley, and U.S. Steel's William White—and each company, as a tax-deductible expense, foots the Carlton Club membership fee of $360 a year for its lobbyist and pays other related expenses.

There are around five thousand lobbyists in Washington. Most of them represent special financial interests. From 1918 until 1962, corporations were not allowed to deduct lobbying expenses from their income taxes. But the Tax "Reform" Act of 1962 changed this. Now these expenses—unlike the efforts of ordinary citizens to affect government policies—*are* tax-deductible. The result is that average taxpayers not only pay more than their fair share of taxes, but they also help pay for the costs of propagandizing themselves and lobbying government against their own interests.

The lobbying power of concentrated industry is not

just the power of size. The big corporations also have enormous power because their operations are so widespread geographically.

Lockheed has great political power, not just because it's big but because it has plants and offices in a large number of states and congressional districts. Whether or not a particular congressional district will benefit directly from building the SST, say, that district's congressman can probably be counted upon to support the SST project if it will benefit the large company that has a facility in his or her district.

This geographic power is a special evil that results from the growth of conglomerates. Conglomerate giants not only have general economic power, but they more than likely have plants and offices of one kind or another located in a large number of states and congressional districts. And they are frequently able to get a congressman or senator in one state or district to support federal programs or subsidies that help their business in another part of the country.

For example, Tenneco is often able to get a congressman in whose district it has an oil and gas facility to support continuation of the farm subsidy program even though it benefits the parent company in a wholly different area of the country. And, conversely, the company is frequently able to get a congressman in a farm district, where its agricultural operations are prominent, to support the oil and gas depletion allowance, important to its operations in some other state.

One of the best examples of how geographic spread helps translate economic power into political power is the Coca-Cola Company. Coke has an exclusive and monopolistic franchise system under which its local dealers have the exclusive right, without competition, to handle its products in a particular, protected area. The Federal Trade Commission in 1972 said that this exclusive franchise system violates federal law and must be ended. The Federal Trade Commission found that consumers pay 30 percent too much—up to $1.5 billion in over-charges—because there is little competition in the retailing of soft-drink products. Federal Trade Commission action to end the exclusive franchise system would bring down the price of soft drinks by as much as three cents on each ten-cent bottle.

Coke is not willing to submit to this ruling, and the company is trying to change the law retroactively—to get an exemption from the antitrust laws. Because of its immense size and geographic spread, Coca-Cola, through its franchised dealers, is able to lobby every senator and every congressman from his or her own district. The company blankets the United States with about nine hundred local franchise bottlers.

The soft-drink battle is still going on in the Congress. But every day increasing numbers of House and Senate members have agreed to cosponsor Coke's bill—not being able to withstand the lobbying of a local dealer.

The Coke franchise case also illustrates how economic power prevents Congress from getting a true picture of an industry. Coke and other major soft-drink companies want Congress to believe that local bottlers are small businessmen, all in agreement against the Federal Trade Commission ruling. The fact is, as the Federal Trade Commission has shown, that the twenty-one largest Coca-Cola bottlers service over one-half of the population of the United States, accounting for about 24 percent of total soft-drink sales. The ten largest Pepsi bottlers serve 45 percent of the population. And truly independent small bottlers are severely restricted in the territories they are allowed to serve.

One of the smaller Coca-Cola bottlers, Mr. Pope Foster of Taft, California, had the courage to come before congressional committees in 1972 to testify against Coke's demand for a retroactive change in the antitrust laws. He wanted to see more competition, the right of each local retail bottler to compete with other bottlers, without protected territories. When he returned home after testifying, as he has said, "The Coca-Cola Company called to tell me that they had gone over their figures and found I had been getting too much syrup, so they were cutting me back to make up for it."

But Mr. Foster is continuing to fight. "Now I feel more strongly than ever that the real facts and issues should not be obscured or suppressed by the smoke screen put up by these powerful men who control the syrup—the lifeblood of the soft-drink industry," he says. Not many independent businessmen are so willing and able to stand up to the powerful economic interests. Neither are very many public officials.

The fundamental problem is concentrated economic power. And this is demonstrated very clearly in the way corporate officials use community involvement to affect public policy.

Corporate officials have time to spend in civic activity. Corporations not only encourage civic involvement, they require it. The corporations see this as one important way they can expand their efforts to affect public opinion.

Utility companies are the best example here. The Public Service Company of Colorado—which is both a gas and electric company—has seen to it that its local officials serve on twenty-two state commissions and on the boards of directors of nineteen local chambers of commerce, nineteen civic organizations (such as the Red Cross), thirty-two business and professional organizations, eight colleges and universities, and five of the ten largest banks in the Denver area.

The president of this giant utility, or his representative, serves on every state commission on economic development, two state environmental authorities, the state highway commission, and the state health and education planning councils.

Because, as the Public Service Company of Colorado says, "we're involved," the utility company is in a position to have the last word in such matters as the rates to be charged, the services to be provided to consumers, and whether or not consumers in some areas will be served at all.

When former Texas Governor John Connally—who has had an almost Siamese-twin relationship with big business throughout his political life—was required by Texas law to appoint a state air pollution control board, he appointed the people who were most closely tied with the industries involved. As a Nader report has shown, he not only appointed corporate executives, who had particular corporate axes to grind, to so-called public positions, but "he filled the industry slot with the most unreconstructed polluter in the state. The man in question, John T. Files, was Secretary-Treasurer of the Texas Chemical Council and President of the Merichem Company, whose plants are easily recognized by the black smoke and sickening odor which come pouring out of the stack." Most other state pollution boards are similarly dominated by industries that are the worst polluters.

The same is true at the federal level. Whenever an important board or commission is to be appointed, the industries and companies concerned are somehow able, whether the Republicans or the Democrats are in power, to convince the President or other appointing powers that "fairness" requires their being represented on such boards or commissions that affect corporate profitability.

Banks—national and local—are the best at this practice. Their officials are always on every board or commission, whether it is set up to consider improved mass transit in New York or better bank regulation at the federal level.

Community involvement is used, too, in reverse, for corporate profit. Corporations regularly demand all sorts of special privileges from local communities—tax advantages and taxpayer financing of special water, sewer, and transportation costs—before they agree to locate in a community. And, at the slightest provocation, they threaten to leave.

General Motors had a plant in Tarrytown, New York, which federal court action proved was in violation of the law against discharging industrial wastes into the Hudson River. GM fired several hundred local employees and made it clear that the balance of the employees in the plant would be discharged, with resulting adverse economic impact in the local area, if residents of the Hudson River Valley pushed too hard for a real cleanup of the river.

Control through community involvement and through threats to local communities if they act in the public interest can be curtailed only by cutting down on concentrated economic power and by requiring that corporations *internalize* their real costs.

The costs of pollution should not be public costs. The costs of runaway plants—unemployed workers and unsupported school systems—should not be public costs. These costs should be among the internal corporate costs of doing business.

When corporations can no longer *externalize* these costs—pass them along to the taxpayers—it will be clearer to the general public why corporations require their officials to become so involved in civic and local affairs. Corporations want ordinary taxpayers to be misled into believing that their interests are the same as corporate interests, that private citizens should subsidize a part of the real costs of the corporations doing business in their areas.

In industry, as in agribusiness, powerful corporations use job interchange as another way of controlling public policy. Officials move, freely and regularly, from industry to government, and from government to industry.

At the state level, for example, consider the Public Service Company of Colorado and the Colorado Public Utility Commission, which is supposed to regulate it. Twenty-seven of the commission's sixty-five-member staff formerly worked for the Public Service Company of Colorado. This number includes the commission's one staff attorney. He worked for the Public Service Company of Colorado for fifteen years before he joined the regulatory commission's staff.

At the federal level, it's worse. Horace Godfrey, whose Department of Agriculture job involved administering the Sugar Act, left the Johnson Administration to become the chief lobbyist for the American Sugar Cane League. Dick Briggs left the staff of the Interstate Commerce Commission in 1969 to become executive director of ASTRO—funded by the Association of American Railroads—which manages railroad efforts for greater federal subsidies. Carl Bagge retired from membership on the Federal Power Commission to become head of the National Coal Administration.

Clifford Hardin resigned as Secretary of Agriculture to become vice-chairman of the Ralston Purina Company, a major agribusiness corporation that benefits from numerous federal programs. And, as we know, Dr. Earl Butz resigned from Ralston Purina's board of directors to become the new Secretary of Agriculture.

It is the rule, rather than the exception, that an executive takes a job with a federal regulatory agency, perhaps moves from there to academia, moves from there to industry, and then moves back to the regulatory agency. The cycle is seldom broken. Job interchange between government and industry is a way of life.

It's no wonder that in 1972 the Federal Communications Commission—whose main congressional mandate calls for regulation of interstate telephone rates—announced that it simply had neither the time nor the money to look into the rate charges by American Telephone & Telegraph Company. When FCC Commissioner Nicholas Johnson joined with the late Congressman William F. Ryan of New York and myself in blowing the whistle on it, the FCC reversed itself. Yes, it said, we will now investigate American Telephone & Telegraph's rate structure. Not many observers were reassured by FCC's change of position. Subsequent history indicates that its announcement was intended mainly to reduce public pressure on itself.

FCC had as its basic congressional mandate, from the very first, a directive to investigate and regulate interstate telephone rates. But, for all these years, it has felt secure in refusing to do so. The Johnson-Harris-Ryan outcry surprised and embarrassed them enough at least to make them announce the proper goal. But in spite of the appearance of activity, essentially nothing has happened.

And nothing is likely to happen. The big corporations, with big economic power, use that power to dominate government. They are particularly adept at dominating government regulations. One avenue they use is the swinging door between industry jobs and regulatory jobs. The fundamental answer is not better regulation—

though that would be an improvement. The answer is government action to break up economic power, so that economic power cannot be translated into concomitant political power. And a reduction in the dependence on government regulation, requiring less reliance on political power through government regulation, will have the best results.

Why don't we hear more about this? Why doesn't the press concentrate more on these basic economic and political issues? I'm often asked these questions.

A part of the answer has to be that the press itself is a concentrated industry. Every time a daily newspaper comes up for sale, some chain buys it. Local newspaper corporations are allowed to pool their printing and advertising departments to avoid competition. Newspaper corporations are supposed to be competitive with television and radio stations, but the joint ownership of them actually prevents real competition. The big networks are corporate conglomerates, engaged in a wide range of industrial activities along with communications.

Twenty-five percent of all television stations are controlled by newspapers. At another level, NBC is owned by RCA Corporation, a huge national conglomerate. Time Inc. is a huge multimedia power. In Oklahoma just four owners control 88 percent of total radio and television income. And telephone companies are moving into cable TV all over America.

Most dailies and most television stations in each of the major cities are owned by chains of one kind or another. It is not Agnewism to say that the news is owned and controlled in America by big corporate interests. It's just the truth. No wonder that these owners, normally vigorous defenders of the public interest, are relatively quiet about the concentration of economic power in this country. They exemplify that concentration in their own operations.

The New Populism

Reforms alone will not do. Better regulation will not really change things enough. Every time the people win a public policy victory, it had better be a victory for structural change in concentrated economic power. Otherwise the victory is transitory and superficial.

One of the greatest of the old populist leaders saw the problem clearly. "I have become more and more impressed with the deep underlying singleness of the issue," Senator Robert La Follette said. "It is not the tariff or conservation or the currency. It is not the trusts. The supreme issue, involving all others, is the encroachment of the powerful few upon the rights of the many."

For problems this big, reforms will not suffice. Unless we are willing to deal with the underlying evils of concentrated economic power, everything else is a snare and a delusion.

EPILOGUE

Power to the People

The New Populism is not a precisely formulated prescription for all nations and all people. It has been developed out of the *American* idiom—and it attempts to deal with the American situation.

The New Populism advocates doing the best we can with what we have to work with. And what we have to work with is considerable: a strong sense of nationhood and cohesiveness as a people; a fundamental tradition of democracy; an announced public philosophy that hinges on individual liberty and equality; a stated goal of economic freedom and opportunity.

We can call this group of ideas the American inheritance. In most instances, the New Populism seeks simply to show America how it must *do* what it *says*. In most instances, too, the legal framework and the necessary institutions for what we must do already exist. Surprisingly little change will be necessary to produce substantial improvement in the effect of our institutions.

The New Populism is a statement that public stability

and individual self-satisfaction in America are a direct result of the degree to which, as a matter of *social contract* with each other, the American people share in the American inheritance.

This social contract has three basic aspects. It is held together, first of all, by the self-interest of each party to the contract in seeing that he himself and the other parties to the contract share fairly in the American inheritance.

The New Populism does not seek the support of an individual citizen merely on the basis of asking him or her to be good to black people or other minorities because Christian teachings, for example, demand such an attitude. It does not ask an individual citizen to agree to allow other people fuller participation in the political process or in economic power merely because it is "morally" right to agree with this.

The New Populism maintains, instead: "It is in your own *self-interest* to agree to these principles of the social contract; otherwise, your own lives and your society are not going to be fully secure and fully satisfying."

Secondly, the social contract depends upon a better distribution of wealth and income and economic power. Absolute equality is not required. But the imbalances must not be so great as to produce political inequality.

Finally, the social contract depends upon widespread participation in decision-making. This is a central element in the American inheritance. Yet participation is hampered today by the pervasive influence of huge concentrations of wealth and income. It is thwarted today, too, by unprecedented and unforeseen concentrations of power in both huge, impersonal economic institutions and huge, remote political institutions.

The people and the policy-makers, then, in order to implement the New Populism, must judge the efficacy and correctness of all decisions and actions in terms of: the self-interest of the people; the participation of the people; and the distributive effect, economically and politically.

People cannot fully "participate" in a centralized federal government of more than 200 million people in an industrialized and urbanized society. But that doesn't mean that we have to become even more elitist than we are. It doesn't mean that the experts should make even more of the important decisions than they now do because the people are, as some liberals seem to believe, incapable of doing so. That kind of attitude puts academic political scientists in charge of foreign policy, for example, and encourages them to make secret decisions.

The growing power of the experts has partly resulted from conservative influence. Protected elites and those who want to become protected elites—be they lawyers, plumbers, accountants, beauticians, social workers, doctors, or shorthand reporters—have pressured government (mostly state governments) to guarantee by law their power and control; and their control often becomes hereditary.

The apathy of the present times, so often decried by politicians and political observers, grows out of a general feeling in the country that ordinary people cannot really participate in decision-making and that, even if they could, the present concentration of power would prevent them from really changing things.

Since participation is a vital part of the social contract, it is imperative that we recognize that making our society work is going to depend upon freer choices and more actual participation. And we must act against present barriers to participation, whether they're inspired by liberal elitists or founded upon conservative protectionism.

But, in any event, real participation will not be possible unless it is also recognized that traditional *political* participation, in the modern context, is insufficient to give ordinary citizens a real share in control.

In the highly industrialized society we have become, workers, for example, cannot be said to be actual participants in decision-making when they have no share in corporate decisions or in control of the places where they work.

Centralized government allows citizen participation only in the process of electing representatives. This is necessary. But it is not satisfactory. One solution—and a vital one—is to decrease the importance of the central government. The easiest way to accomplish this is to eliminate those government intrusions into our private lives which are neither warranted by results nor justified by the goals they're supposed to achieve.

Ready examples come to mind. It was certainly an elitist who thought up the idea that the government should spy on its own people.

Conservatives, who profess to be civil libertarians, in the sense of being pro-individual and anti–big government—have forced through laws that allow widespread government surveillance of ordinary citizens. And they sanction other largely unrestricted government invasions of individual privacy.

Preventive detention laws, the power of authorities to break and enter in certain circumstances, and, as some government officials claim, the inherent right of government to listen in on private conversations—all these undermine the American inheritance.

The same basic issue is involved, too, in more controversial subjects. The government has enough to do without involving itself in the private sexual acts of its citizens, homosexual or otherwise. It has no business telling people what they can read. And it should not coerce individuals through a peacetime military draft, as President Nixon's action recognizes. Those who advocate such unnecessary interference in people's private lives are advocating elitist concepts.

Making criminals out of people who use marijuana—a drug that's been found no more harmful than alcohol—also grows out of an elitist attempt to use the government to enforce a general system of morals on its citizens. Even conservative William F. Buckley's *National Review* has taken a civil libertarian stand against present marijuana laws.

Medical realities and the well-established legal rights of an unborn child, when it has developed enough to survive and is therefore considered a "person" under the law—as the U.S. Supreme Court has recently ruled—are sufficient in themselves to decide the question of abortion, without government involvement in what is a matter of conscience between a woman and her own doctor. There is no excuse to abrogate the civil right of a woman to control her own body.

It has been said that these are political issues that are too hot to handle. But these issues must be dealt with by politicians, because they are real issues. The New Populism seeks to put them in the proper context, in terms of the American inheritance and the underlying social contract that enforces it.

When government is called upon to do something, it ought to *act*, rather than merely say something or start another program. What the government does should result in structural changes, so that natural forces, rather than a simple faith in government, can operate freely to enforce announced goals. The government ought to act against inordinate concentrations of power, so that competition will itself have a self-regulating and distributive effect.

Also, when government acts, it should act to treat causes rather than symptoms. More often than not, an asserted need for a government social program really results from a lack of money in the hands of the citizens who are said to need help. I saw something lately that indicated that former Secretary of Housing and Urban Development George Romney has come around to the view that we would be better off to provide *money* for people who need housing, rather than just housing programs. If that's his view, he's on the right track. People who do not have good housing are prevented from getting it for two reasons: they lack the money to buy it; or they are barred from getting it by racial considerations or by the costs resulting from government-imposed zoning and government-imposed restrictions on competition in the building trades.

By treating symptoms and ignoring causes, government housing programs have often increased the segregation of low-income people in areas where there are no jobs, increased the segregation of old people in enclaves where they have no general contact with other age groups, increased the segregation of black people on the basis of race.

And, on top of all this, government housing programs have tended to ignore the basic principle of participation. Housing users and occupants are denied full participation in the decisions that govern a large part of their lives. They are not taken into full account in the system of governance of public housing in which they live.

Participation is also denied in education. Students could share more in the control of education if they had money. Basically, this kind of participation would result from an economic system in which income and wealth were more fairly distributed. Past that, it would result from putting cash—or the equivalents of cash—in the hands of the students themselves, rather than into the treasuries of institutions. And education programs ought also to build in a requirement that the consumers of education participate in political control of their schools.

Too many young people are made idle and are alienated by a system that forces them today to live apart from the processes that govern their lives. Students are citizens too. There's no inherent reason why government officials and education administrators should constitute an elite that rules the whole educational community. The students and the faculty constitute an essential part of that community. They should not be ruled by undemocratic fiat or decree.

The Bureau of Indian Affairs is a classic example of how government treats symptoms rather than causes. American Indians rank at the bottom of just about every measurement of social and economic well-being. Why? Because they don't have money, and they lack control. The Bureau of Indian Affairs is an elitist organization. Even when Native Americans are brought into its Washington operations, the bureau still tends to exemplify the belief that government knows better than the people themselves what should be done.

Additional power and participation for Native Americans could be achieved almost overnight simply by cutting the Washington staff of the Bureau of Indian Affairs by at least one-half. Indians have a hard time bearing up under the present burden of bureaucratic superstructure. And government programs for Indian education, housing, health, jobs, and welfare ought to be turned over to Native Americans. Let them run their own programs.

Next to tax justice, health—the failure in America's health delivery system and the inability of ordinary people to pay for health care—is probably the most important populist issue in the country. Under the present non-system, doctors control health delivery.

Doctors earn a median income of more than $40,000 a year. They are the highest paid profession in America. And they want to keep their high income. Doctors help keep medical schools from turning out more doctors. And many hospital boards are controlled by doctors who decide which doctors can practice in the hospitals. The doctors who try to cut their fees or who take part in prepaid group medical care plans are not very popular with these doctor-dominated hospital boards.

Doctors help prevent paraprofessionals from achieving full professional status, and they use their influence to prevent an increase in the number of paraprofessionals. There is no reason why there might not be more certified midwives, for example, except that doctors oppose increasing the numbers.

Doctors dominate private health payment plans, such as Blue Cross–Blue Shield. As a matter of fact, they dominate the present government payments plans—Medicare and Medicaid.

The New Populism seeks to spotlight three fundamental aspects of the health delivery problem in America. If these major flaws are not recognized, government policies or programs will merely continue to treat symptoms and not really change things. First of all, most people do not have adequate health care because they can't afford it, because they do not have money.

Secondly, there's a doctors' monopoly over health care delivery. This has to be broken.

Thirdly, professional experts control health care exclusively. Consumers must be given a share in control.

New national health insurance programs must be gauged by all these criteria, and particular attention must be given to their distributive effect.

Where government programs are necessary to meet social problems, the programs ought to be made self-executing whenever possible. The continuing effectiveness of the programs should not depend alone upon the good faith of the government officials who are appointed or otherwise selected to administer them. One of the best tests of a just and workable government is whether or not ordinary people have access to the courts; can lawyers make a living actually doing good?

The monopoly control that lawyers have on the law profession should be broken, or at least opened up through the elimination of published "minimum fee schedules." People ought to be able to shop around.

More importantly, ordinary people's access to the law should not depend solely upon legal fees provided by private charities or the government. As we've seen, anytime lawyers who are paid in this way make too many waves, the tendency of the charity or the government is to cut off the funds that finance such legal services.

The original antipoverty law stated that one of its purposes was to provide funds to poor people for legal advice and advocacy. This sounded very nice, but from the beginning the rhetoric was not matched by the funding. And anytime these government-paid lawyers sued the government or a powerful economic interest, they caused a political backlash. And legal service funds were subsequently cut off or diminished.

There are plenty of precedents for ordinary people to be allowed to recoup their attorneys' fees and costs—and even to get punitive damage awards—for filing lawsuits to force powerful interests, government and economic, to obey the law. They can bring class actions, for themselves and others in their situation, and if they win, they can recover attorneys' fees and special damages from those who engage in illegal conspiracies to set prices. They can do something similar in antitrust suits.

In 1972 the Senate passed—but the House killed—a new consumer product safety bill that did not depend upon the good faith of government administrators. The idea embodied in this Senate bill was that ordinary citizens should be reimbursed for their attorneys' fees and costs in bringing actions against corporations to enforce this new product safety act. And they should be able to recover attorney fees and costs for bringing actions against relevant government agencies, in order to require them to do their legal duty and enforce the law.

This is the direction—self-enforcement—in which new government policies and programs must go. It doesn't help much to adopt a new program for consumer protection if President Nixon can appoint those who will administer it. It doesn't help much to enact a new federal law requiring huge interstate corporations to be chartered at the federal level if conservative interests can dictate the appointment of those who will enforce the law.

Laws and programs must be made self-executing, so far as possible. It's not enough to provide, for the moment, taxpayer funds to assist ordinary litigants in paying their attorneys' fees and costs. Such monies are too easily cut off. New programs ought to make structural changes to give ordinary citizens real access to the courts, by allowing them to recover lawyers' fees, costs, and damages for going into court to enforce what has been determined to be the public interest.

And we must break down local government into manageable units in which ordinary people can have some real say.

The frustrations of Americans who live in cities are not limited to the New Yorker who must compete with nearly eight million other citizens for the attention of his or her local government. Many American cities have given up on participatory governmental structures. From the early 1900s on, these cities embraced a system that vested city power in one technician, a city manager.

One reason why the city manager form of government was adopted in so many American cities was that city councils were elected at large—a system that prevented popular control. At-large election of city councilmen means that an ordinary citizen is not directly represented at city hall. There's no direct recourse to one's representative. And this system, where adopted, has generally meant that a black minority has little, if any, influence on city hall.

The idea of the city manager form of government and of the citywide election of city councilmen stemmed from the elitist notion that government will be better if it is removed from politics, farther from popular control.

A related elitism causes New York City, and many other American cities, to be governed by one central government with little popular power or control over policies by neighborhoods. In these large cities, it is reasonable to provide citywide jurisdiction for taxation and for basic governmental services. But it is unreasonable to centralize in one city hall control over the delivery of services that can easily be decentralized to the neighborhood level—law enforcement and garbage collection, for example.

For it is an obvious rule of government that the greater the number of bureaucratic steps between ordinary people and their officials, the slower will be action taken to deal with problems.

New York City tried to deal with this situation by setting up little city halls. It didn't work. Similar efforts, funded by the federal Model Cities and related programs, to decentralize government control in other cities didn't work either. Neighborhoods were given no actual control. The neighborhood should really be allowed to select and control the officials who administer neighborhood programs—police protection and garbage collection, for example.

But how does this square with busing? If neighborhoods are to be given real control over essential services, why should they not have control over neighborhood schools? Neighborhoods *should* control their own schools—unless neighborhood control really amounts to racial discrimination and inequality of educational opportunity. In this instance, the more fundamental promise of the American inheritance for equality before the law must take precedence.

Court-ordered busing of schoolchildren can be made more understandable if people know that it is a stop-gap measure and that there is an alternative that permits neighborhood control. That alternative, advocated by the New Populism, calls for knocking down the racial and class barriers to housing, so that people can live where they want to live. And it calls for evening up the imbalances in wealth and income, so that people can afford quality education wherever they live.

But the real test of a political movement is at the polls. Can the New Populism win on the issues of a better distribution of wealth, income, and power? I believe that the answer can be found in many of the 1972 campaigns around the country that focused on one or more of these issues.

Dan Walker was elected governor of Illinois because of his opposition to Mayor Richard Daley of Chicago. Walker took his campaign directly to the people. Tax reform was a key issue in the successful South Dakota Senate campaign of Jim Abourezk. The tax reform issue was also a crucial reason for the defeat of Senators Margaret Chase Smith of Maine, Gordon Allott of Colorado, and Caleb Boggs of Delaware.

But what about Senator McGovern's losing presidential campaign? The fact that Abourezk won in South Dakota and Walker won in Illinois, while Senator McGovern lost in both states, is instructive. Senator McGovern lost, not *because* he made people's issues the main issues in his campaign, but because he did *not* do so. During and after the Democratic Convention, many people, rightly or wrongly—and it was some of both— came to see Senator McGovern as a person who either did not know his own mind or was willing to change his mind for political reasons. His campaign never recovered.

The people will respond to straight talk and common sense. If given a real choice, the people will see that their own self-interest lies in building a stable society. And they will see that stable societies are more than paper structures, that they depend upon enforcing a general agreement—a social contract—between all the participants in that society. For I believe that people *are* smart enough to govern themselves.

"Power to the people," then, is more than a slogan. It's both an ideal and a necessity.